marie claire
fresh + easy

marie claire
fresh + easy

SIMPLE FOOD FOR RELAXED EATING

Michele Cranston

MURDOCH BOOKS

contents

Laidback weekends, relaxing with friends—that's what this book is about.

When I first started writing these recipes I imagined a beautiful garden filled with springtime blossoms, citrus trees and a wonderfully abundant vegetable plot. I wanted to invoke a nostalgia for simpler times when gardens, friends and food were what good times were all about.

I recalled fond memories of visiting my great aunt's amazing garden, or rummaging through my grandfather's backyard veggie patch.

Then I thought about the food you would be inspired to cook and eat in that environment. I added a

little spice to the food, to balance the sweet and give extra warmth to the meals, and I had fun with the desserts. I knew that the food had to be generous but light, flavoursome but easy, relaxing and delicious.

That meant large platters for lunchtime sharing, laden with fresh garden vegetables and dips, spicy seafood and zesty bites. Pretty afternoon teas with biscuits dusted in icing sugar, richly flavoured cakes and summery desserts. Old-fashioned tablecloths covered with sweets bursting with the flavours of citrus, blossom and vanilla. And hearty meals with earthy aromas for winter warmth.

With such lush greenery in the garden, there would naturally be steamed vegetables, comforting soups and zen-inspired noodles and broths as well.

And since my vision was all about being relaxed around food, the recipes are, as always, simple and time-friendly. It's all about having fun with food and enjoying fresh flavours and easy cooking.

bite

early morning tasty bites

BOILED EGGS WITH DUKKAH
FETA AND SPINACH FRITTERS
BAKED MUSHROOMS AND GRUYERE ON TOAST
ZUCCHINI AND LEMON FRITTATA
CORNBREAD
TOMATOES WITH PROSCIUTTO, BASIL AND OLIVES
DATE AND COCONUT BARS
RASPBERRY BROWN SUGAR MUFFINS
CINNAMON SWIRLS
CHOCOLATE BRAN MUFFINS

boiled eggs with dukkah

50 g (1¾ oz/½ cup) flaked almonds
40 g (1½ oz/¼ cup) sesame seeds
2 teaspoons coriander seeds
1 tablespoon cumin seeds
2 teaspoons sumac
½ teaspoon freshly ground black pepper
½ teaspoon sea salt
4 boiled eggs, to serve

Preheat the oven to 180°C (350°F/Gas 4).

Spread the flaked almonds over a baking tray and put them in the oven for 5 minutes or until golden brown. Remove from the oven and allow to cool.

Put the roasted almonds in a food processor with the sesame seeds, coriander seeds, cumin seeds, sumac, black pepper and sea salt. Pulse to form rough crumbs.

Serve with boiled eggs.

SERVES 4

feta and spinach fritters

1 bunch (350 g/12 oz) English spinach,
    trimmed and rinsed
3 eggs
150 g (5½ oz/1 cup) self-raising flour
100 g (3½ oz/⅔ cup) feta cheese, crumbled
4 shallots, finely sliced
¼ teaspoon ground nutmeg
6 mint leaves, finely sliced
2 tablespoons vegetable oil for cooking
lemon wedges, to serve

Heat a large frying pan over medium heat. Put the spinach into the
pan and cover with a lid. Cook for 3–4 minutes, turning occasionally
until the spinach is dark green. Remove from the heat and allow the
spinach to cool. Remove any excess liquid from the spinach,
then finely chop it.

Put the eggs and flour in a bowl and whisk to combine. Add the
chopped spinach, feta cheese, shallots, nutmeg and mint, and mix
well. Season to taste with sea salt and freshly ground black pepper.

Heat a little vegetable oil in a frying pan over medium to high heat
and drop heaped tablespoons of fritter mixture into the pan.
Cook until golden brown on one side, then flip over and cook for a
further 2 minutes. Remove to a warm tray and cook the remaining
mixture, adding a little more oil as required.

Serve warm with wedges of lemon.

MAKES 12

baked mushrooms and gruyere on toast

24 vine leaves in brine
12 medium-sized flat field or portobello mushrooms, stalks removed
12 sprigs thyme
6 whole garlic cloves
125 ml (4 fl oz/½ cup) extra virgin olive oil
4 slices sourdough bread, toasted
4–8 thin slices gruyère cheese

Preheat the oven to 180°C (350°F/Gas 4).

Lightly rinse the vine leaves and arrange half of them in the base of a ceramic baking dish. Arrange the mushrooms over the vine leaves with the thyme sprigs. Using the flat side of a large knife, crush the garlic cloves and put them into the dish around the mushrooms. Drizzle the extra virgin olive oil over the mushrooms, then cover with the remaining vine leaves. Cover the baking dish with a lid or foil.

Bake in the oven for 1 hour.

Put the four slices of toasted sourdough onto four plates and top with the gruyère cheese. Arrange the hot mushrooms over the top and drizzle with some of the warm cooking juices.

SERVES 4

zucchini and lemon frittata

40 g (1½ oz) butter
1 onion, finely chopped
1 tablespoon roughly chopped
   marjoram
3 medium zucchini (courgettes), grated
6 eggs
1 teaspoon finely grated lemon zest
150 g (5½ oz) firm ricotta cheese
35 g (1¼ oz/⅓ cup) finely grated
   parmesan cheese

Preheat the oven to 180°C (350°F/Gas 4).

Heat a large ovenproof frying pan over
medium heat and add the butter, onion
and marjoram. Cook until the onion is soft,
then add the zucchini. Cook for a further
5 minutes, stirring occasionally.

Whisk the eggs and grated lemon
zest together and season with sea salt
and freshly ground black pepper. Pour
the eggs over the zucchini mix, top
with teaspoonfuls of the ricotta cheese,
then sprinkle the grated parmesan
cheese over.

Bake in the oven for 10 minutes or until
puffed up and golden brown.

Remove, and serve with a green salad
or buttery toast.

SERVES 6

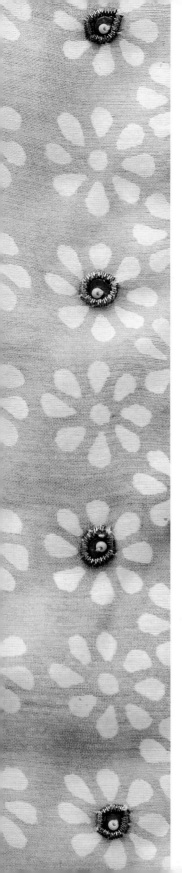

cornbread

150 g (5½ oz/1 cup) polenta
75 g (2½ oz/½ cup) plain (all-purpose) flour
1 tablespoon baking powder
1 tablespoon sugar
1 teaspoon paprika
115 g (4 oz/¾ cup) diced green capsicum (pepper)
2 corn cobs, kernels removed
5 spring onions (scallions), finely sliced
1 bunch coriander (cilantro), roughly chopped
3 eggs, lightly beaten
250 ml (9 fl oz/1 cup) buttermilk
170 ml (5½ fl oz/⅔ cup) olive oil
125 g (4½ oz/1 cup) goat's cheese
½ teaspoon chilli flakes

Preheat the oven to 180°C (350°F/Gas 4).

Grease a 20 x 30 cm (8 x 12 in) baking tin and line it with
baking paper.

In a bowl combine the polenta, flour, baking powder, sugar and
paprika. Add the green capsicum (pepper), corn kernels, spring onions
(scallions) and coriander (cilantro) and mix well. Season with sea salt
and freshly ground black pepper.

In a separate bowl, whisk together the eggs, buttermilk and olive oil,
then stir the liquid into the dry ingredients. Mix well, then pour the
batter into the prepared tin and crumble the goat's cheese over the
top. Sprinkle with chilli flakes. Bake for 35 minutes or until a skewer
comes out clean when inserted into the centre.

Cut into six squares and serve with roasted tomatoes and
coriander sprigs.

SERVES 6

tomatoes with prosciutto, basil and olives

4 large vine-ripened tomatoes
2 slices sourdough bread, crusts removed
8 basil leaves, roughly torn
12 kalamata olives, pitted and roughly chopped
2 tablespoons finely chopped parsley
2 tablespoons finely grated parmesan cheese
2 tablespoons extra virgin olive oil, plus extra to serve
4 slices prosciutto
2 handfuls baby rocket (arugula) leaves

Preheat the oven to 180°C (350°F/Gas 4).

Slice the top from each of the tomatoes and set them aside.

Using a small spoon, scoop the flesh out of each of the tomatoes and put it in a bowl. Tear the bread into small chunks and add it to the bowl along with the basil leaves, olives, parsley, parmesan cheese and extra virgin olive oil. Stir to combine, then spoon the flavoured mixture back into the centre of each of the tomatoes.

Wrap a slice of prosciutto around one of the tomatoes, starting at the top, covering the base and returning to the top. Seal with the 'hat' of the tomato. Put the tomato into a shallow baking tin, and repeat with the remaining three tomatoes.

Bake in the oven for 25–30 minutes.

Serve on a bed of baby rocket leaves with a drizzle of extra virgin olive oil.

SERVES 4

date and coconut bars

165 g (5¾ oz/1 cup) chopped dates
185 g (6½ oz/1 cup) soft brown sugar
60 g (2¼ oz/1 cup) shredded coconut
100 g (3½ oz/1 cup) rolled (porridge)
   oats
40 g (1½ oz/¼ cup) linseeds (flax
   seeds)
150 g (5½ oz/1 cup) self-raising flour
225 g (8 oz) butter
2 large tablespoons golden syrup

Preheat the oven to 160°C (315°F/Gas 2–3).

Grease a 20 x 30 cm (8 x 12 in) baking tin.

Put the dates, brown sugar, coconut, oats,
linseeds and flour into a large mixing bowl
and toss several times until well combined.

Melt the butter and golden syrup in a small
saucepan and pour the mixture over the
dry ingredients. Stir until well combined.

Pour the mixture into the prepared tin
and bake for 40 minutes. Allow to cool
before slicing into bars. Store in an
airtight container.

MAKES 12 PIECES

raspberry brown sugar muffins

250 g (9 oz/1⅔ cups) plain (all-purpose) flour
150 g (5½ oz/¾ cup) soft brown sugar
½ teaspoon bicarbonate of soda (baking soda)
½ teaspoon salt
150 g (5½ oz/1¼ cups) frozen raspberries
80 ml (2½ fl oz/⅓ cup) vegetable oil
1 egg
200 ml (7 fl oz) buttermilk
1 teaspoon natural vanilla extract
70 g (2½ oz/⅓ cup) raw (demerara) sugar
½ teaspoon ground cinnamon

Preheat the oven to 180°C (350°F/Gas 4).

Grease eight holes of a standard muffin tin or line with paper cases.

Combine the flour, brown sugar, bicarbonate of soda and salt in
a large bowl, then toss the raspberries through the dry ingredients.

In a separate bowl whisk together the oil, egg, buttermilk and vanilla
extract. Pour the liquid ingredients over the dry ingredients and stir
until they have just come together. Do not over-mix.

Spoon the batter into the prepared muffin tin and top with the raw
sugar and cinnamon. Bake for 20–25 minutes or until the muffins are
cooked through. Remove to a wire rack and allow the muffins to cool.

MAKES 8

cinnamon swirls

60 ml (2 fl oz/¼ cup) milk, plus a little extra for glazing
7 g (1 sachet) dry yeast
300 g (10½ oz/2 cups) plain (all-purpose) flour
2 tablespoons sugar
2 large eggs, whisked
100 g (3½ oz) butter, melted
1 teaspoon sea salt
165 g (5¾ oz/¾ cup) caster (superfine) sugar
3 teaspoons ground cinnamon
2 tablespoons poppy seeds (optional)

Preheat the oven to 180°C (350°F/Gas 4).

Heat the milk in a small saucepan until it is lukewarm. Remove from the heat and pour into a bowl, then sprinkle the yeast and 35 g (1¼ oz/¼ cup) of the flour over the milk. Stir to combine, then cover and allow to sit for 10 minutes or until the mixture looks as if it is beginning to bubble.

Add the remaining flour, sugar, eggs, melted butter and sea salt. Stir to combine, then turn out onto a lightly floured surface. Knead the dough until it is smooth and elastic, then put it into a lightly oiled bowl. Cover and allow to sit in a warm place for an hour or until the dough has doubled in size.

Punch the dough down and put it on a large piece of baking paper. Roughly flatten the dough, lightly flour its surface, then roll it with a rolling pin until the dough is approximately 30 x 45 cm (12 x 17¾ in). Combine the caster (superfine) sugar and the ground cinnamon and sprinkle over the dough. Roll the dough up widthways to form a long Swiss roll. Cut into 2 cm (¾ in) slices and put the slices onto a baking tray lined with baking paper. Cover with a clean tea towel (dish towel) and allow to rise for half an hour. Brush the sliced dough with a little milk and, if you like, sprinkle with poppy seeds. Bake in the oven for 15–20 minutes.

Serve warm.

MAKES 15

chocolate bran muffins

250 g (9 oz/1 cup) plain yoghurt
100 ml (3½ fl oz) vegetable oil
2 eggs
2 teaspoons natural vanilla extract
335 g (11¾ oz/2¼ cups) plain (all-purpose) flour
1 tablespoon baking powder
2 tablespoons dark cocoa powder
35 g (1¼ oz/¼ cup) oat bran
½ teaspoon ground cinnamon
185 g (6½ oz/1 cup) soft brown sugar
2 green apples, grated

cranberry butter
100 g (3½ oz/1 cup) dried cranberries
100 g (3½ oz) butter, softened

Preheat the oven to 180°C (350°F/Gas 4).

Grease twelve holes of a standard muffin tin or line with paper cases.

Put the yoghurt, vegetable oil, eggs and vanilla extract in a bowl and whisk to combine.

Sift the flour, baking powder and cocoa powder into a large bowl and add the oat bran, cinnamon, brown sugar and grated apple. Stir well so that the apple is well incorporated into the dry ingredients. Pour the liquid ingredients over the dry ingredients and stir until they have just come together. Do not over-mix.

Spoon the mixture into the prepared muffin tin. Bake for 30 minutes or until the tops feel firm and a skewer inserted into the centre comes out clean.

Meanwhile, to make the cranberry butter, put the cranberries and softened butter into a food processor and blend until the cranberries have worked their way into the butter. Spoon the flavoured butter onto a piece of baking paper and roll up to form a log. Refrigerate. Serve the muffins warm with the cranberry butter.

MAKES 12

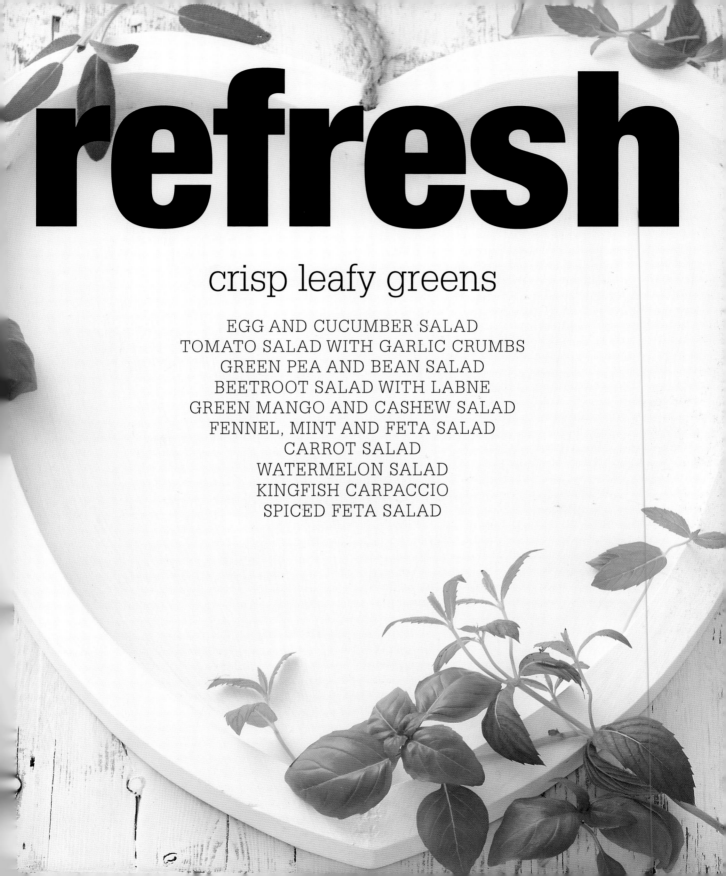

refresh

crisp leafy greens

EGG AND CUCUMBER SALAD
TOMATO SALAD WITH GARLIC CRUMBS
GREEN PEA AND BEAN SALAD
BEETROOT SALAD WITH LABNE
GREEN MANGO AND CASHEW SALAD
FENNEL, MINT AND FETA SALAD
CARROT SALAD
WATERMELON SALAD
KINGFISH CARPACCIO
SPICED FETA SALAD

egg and cucumber salad

4 fresh coriander (cilantro) roots, rinsed
1 large garlic clove, crushed
1 birdseye chilli, finely chopped
1 teaspoon soft brown sugar
1 teaspoon sea salt
2 tablespoons lime juice
125 ml (4 fl oz/½ cup) olive oil
4 Lebanese (short) cucumbers
½ red onion, finely diced
30 g (1 oz/1 cup) picked chervil leaves
30 g (1 oz/1 cup) picked coriander (cilantro) leaves
10 g (¼ oz/½ cup) picked mint leaves
10 chives, snipped
4 hard-boiled eggs, peeled
30 g (1 oz) pine nuts, toasted

To make the dressing, finely chop the coriander (cilantro) roots and combine with the garlic, chilli, sugar and sea salt. Add the lime juice and olive oil, whisk to combine and set aside.

Chop the cucumbers into chunks and combine with the onion and herbs in a bowl. Pour the dressing over the cucumber mix and lightly toss.

Arrange the dressed salad on a platter. Roughly chop the eggs and sprinkle them over the salad with the toasted pine nuts.

SERVES 4

tomato salad with garlic crumbs

2 slices sourdough bread, crusts removed
2 garlic cloves
½ teaspoon sea salt
1 teaspoon finely chopped rosemary
2 tablespoons olive oil
6 large vine-ripened tomatoes
2 tablespoons finely chopped parsley
1 tablespoon extra virgin olive oil
1 teaspoon red wine vinegar
1 tablespoon small salted capers, rinsed

Preheat the oven to 180°C (350°F/Gas 4).

Put the bread, garlic, sea salt and rosemary into a food processor with some freshly ground black pepper and pulse to form breadcrumbs. Add the extra virgin olive oil and pulse a few more times.

Spread the breadcrumbs over a baking tray and bake in the oven until golden. Remove, and allow to cool.

Cut the tomatoes into bite-sized chunks, season with sea salt and freshly ground black pepper, and arrange on a serving platter. Top with the parsley. Whisk the extra virgin olive oil and the vinegar together and drizzle over the salad.

Toss the salted capers through the breadcrumbs and scatter them over the tomato salad.

SERVES 4–6 AS A SIDE DISH

green pea and bean salad

1 tablespoon lemon juice
60 ml (2 fl oz/¼ cup) extra virgin
   olive oil
100 g (3½ oz/1⅓ cups) sugar
   snap peas
100 g (3½ oz/⅔ cup) green peas
150 g (5½ oz) green beans
50 g (1¾ oz) pine nuts, toasted
zest of 1 lemon
2 tablespoons roughly chopped
   flat-leaf (Italian) parsley

Put the lemon juice and extra virgin olive oil in a small bowl. Season with a little sea salt and freshly ground black pepper and whisk to combine.

Bring a saucepan of salted water to the boil and blanch the peas and beans until they turn emerald green. Drain, and refresh under cold running water, then toss in the dressing and arrange on a serving plate.

Top with the pine nuts, lemon zest and parsley.

SERVES 4 AS A SIDE DISH

beetroot salad with labne

4 medium-sized beetroot (beets)
2 tablespoons olive oil
1 tablespoon sumac
1 tablespoon lemon thyme leaves
30 g (1 oz/1 cup) roughly chopped
   flat-leaf (Italian) parsley
1 bunch chives, snipped
juice of 1 lemon
200 g (7 oz) labne (see extras,
   page 242)

Preheat the oven to 200°C (400°F/Gas 6).

Wearing rubber gloves, peel the beetroots and cut them into bite-sized chunks. Put the chunks into a bowl with the olive oil, sumac and lemon thyme, and toss to ensure that the beetroot is well coated in the flavoured oil.

Transfer the beetroot chunks to a baking tin and cover with a lid or foil. Bake in the oven for 30 minutes or until the beetroot is cooked through. Remove and allow to cool.

Put the beetroot into a bowl with the herbs and toss well. Spoon into a serving bowl and top with spoonfuls of the labne.

SERVES 4 AS A SIDE DISH

green mango and cashew salad

2 tablespoons light olive oil
1 teaspoon brown mustard seeds
100 g (3½ oz) shallots, peeled, halved and sliced
¼ teaspoon dried red chilli flakes
¼ teaspoon ground turmeric
2 tablespoons lemon juice
2 tablespoons apple cider vinegar
1 Lebanese (short) cucumber, diced
2 green mangoes, peeled and flesh julienned
80 g (2¾ oz/½ cup) dry-roasted cashew nuts

Heat the olive oil in a small saucepan and add the mustard seeds.
Continue to cook until the seeds begin to pop. Add the shallots and
stir-fry for several minutes until the shallots are shiny and beginning
to soften. Add the chilli flakes, turmeric and a little sea salt, then add
the lemon juice and vinegar and stir to combine. Remove from the
heat and pour into a large bowl. Allow to cool.

Add the cucumber, mango and cashews and toss until the mango
is well coated.

Serve with pan-fried pork cutlets or barbecued chicken.

SERVES 4 AS A SIDE DISH

fennel, mint and feta salad

2 fennel bulbs, trimmed
juice and grated zest of 2 lemons
80 ml (2½ fl oz/⅓ cup) extra virgin olive oil
2 celery stalks, finely sliced
40 mint leaves, roughly chopped
100 g (3½ oz/⅔ cup) feta cheese, crumbled

Cut the fennel bulbs in half lengthways, then cut them into paper-thin slices. Put the sliced fennel in a bowl and season it with a little sea salt and freshly ground black pepper. Add the lemon juice, lemon zest and extra virgin olive oil and toss well to ensure that the fennel is well coated in the dressing.

Add the celery and mint, and toss once more. Spoon into a serving bowl and top with the crumbled feta cheese.

SERVES 4 AS A SIDE DISH

carrot salad

1 tablespoon light olive oil
1 tablespoon mustard seeds
2 long red chillies, seeded, and sliced on the diagonal
2 tablespoons finely grated fresh ginger
1 garlic clove, peeled and finely chopped
30 g (1 oz/¼ cup) grated palm sugar (jaggery)
1 teaspoon fish sauce
juice of 2 limes
500 g (1 lb 2 oz) carrots
10 mint leaves, sliced

Heat the olive oil in a small saucepan until hot. Add the mustard
seeds and cook until they pop. Add the chillies, ginger and garlic
and cook for a further 2 minutes. Remove from the heat and
add the palm sugar (jaggery), fish sauce and lime juice.
Pour into a bowl and allow to cool.

Peel the carrots and grate them. Add the grated carrot to the
dressing with the sliced mint leaves. Toss to combine.

Serve with barbecued chicken or grilled fish.

SERVES 4 AS A SIDE DISH

watermelon salad

1 red onion
1 tablespoon sea salt
1 teaspoon caster (superfine) sugar
juice of 1 lemon
1 kg (2 lb 4 oz) seedless watermelon
1 Lebanese (short) cucumber, diced
2 teaspoons sumac
10 mint leaves, roughly torn
lime halves, to serve

Peel the onion, cut it in half and finely slice
it into half moons. Put the onion in a bowl
and add the sea salt. Toss several times to
ensure the onion is well coated, then cover
and set aside for 30 minutes.

Drain the onion, then rinse under cold
running water and squeeze out any
excess liquid. Put the onion in a clean
bowl and add the sugar and lemon juice.
Stir to combine, then set aside for a
further 30 minutes.

Remove the rind from the watermelon
and cut the flesh into 2 cm (¾ in) chunks.
Arrange the watermelon and cucumber
on a serving platter and sprinkle with
the sumac and mint leaves. Top with the
pickled onion and serve with lime halves.

SERVES 4 AS A SIDE DISH

kingfish carpaccio

400 g (14 oz) fillet kingfish, sashimi quality
2 tablespoons lime juice
2 tablespoons mirin
1 teaspoon soy sauce
1 heaped tablespoon finely chopped jalapeno peppers
¼ teaspoon smoky paprika

Using a very sharp knife, cut the kingfish into paper-thin slices.
Divide the fish slices between four serving plates, or arrange on
a large serving platter.

In a small bowl, combine the lime juice, mirin and soy sauce.

Spoon the dressing over the fish and scatter with the chopped
jalapeno peppers. Sprinkle with the paprika and serve.

SERVES 4

spiced feta salad

125 ml (4 fl oz/½ cup) olive oil
2 garlic cloves, crushed
2 red chillies, seeded and finely chopped
juice of 2 lemons
1 teaspoon dried oregano
1 baby cos lettuce, finely sliced
a handful of flat-leaf (Italian) parsley,
roughly chopped
10 mint leaves, finely sliced
1 red capsicum (pepper), diced
3 roma (plum) tomatoes, cut into chunks
200 g (7 oz) creamy feta cheese, cut
into small cubes
150 g (5½ oz) small black olives

Put the olive oil, garlic, chillies,
lemon juice and oregano in a small
bowl. Stir to combine.

Put the lettuce and herbs into a
large serving bowl. Top with the red
capsicum (pepper) and tomatoes, then
scatter with the feta cheese and olives.
Drizzle with the dressing and serve.

SERVES 4–6

savour

shared nibbles, platters and dips

SPICED CRUDITES WITH A TARATOR SAUCE
SKEWERED CHILLI PRAWNS
EGGPLANT DIP WITH POMEGRANATE SEEDS
CRAB AND CELERIAC REMOULADE ON LONG TOAST
SALMON CEVICHE
SPICED SARDINES
CHILLI POTATOES
SALT AND PEPPER ALMONDS
CITRUS-SCENTED OLIVES AND CAPERBERRIES
PIQUANT BUFFALO MOZZARELLA BITES

spiced crudites with a tarator sauce

TARATOR SAUCE

2 slices sourdough bread, crusts removed
60 g (2¼ oz) pine nuts, lightly toasted
1 garlic clove
80 ml (2½ fl oz/⅓ cup) lemon juice
60 ml (2 fl oz/¼ cup) olive oil

1 bunch baby carrots, trimmed and peeled
1 bunch radishes, trimmed
1 fennel bulb, trimmed and cut into strips
2 celery stalks, trimmed and cut into sticks
2 Lebanese (short) cucumbers, cut into strips
1 tablespoon sumac
½ teaspoon red chilli flakes

Soak the bread in cold water and squeeze it dry.

Put the bread, pine nuts, garlic, lemon juice and olive oil in a food processor and whiz to form a smooth paste, then add water (about 2 tablespoons) to create a suitable consistency.

Arrange the vegetables on a serving platter and sprinkle with the sumac and chilli flakes. Serve with a bowl of the tarator sauce.

SERVES 4–6 AS AN ENTREE

skewered chilli prawns

2 garlic cloves, crushed
4 bottled jalapeno peppers, finely chopped
juice of 1 lime
1 teaspoon dried oregano
1 teaspoon ground cumin
1 teaspoon ground red chilli
1 teaspoon honey
2 tablespoons olive oil
24 green prawns, peeled and deveined
fresh lime quarters, to serve

Soak 24 small skewers in water for half an hour.

Put the garlic, jalapeno peppers, lime juice, oregano, cumin, red chilli
and honey into a bowl with the olive oil and stir to combine. Season
to taste with sea salt and freshly ground black pepper.

Put one prawn on each skewer and place them in a flat-based
container. Pour the marinade over the prawns and marinate for
half an hour.

Season the prawns with a little sea salt and cook them over a hot
barbecue grill or in a hot oven for 2–3 minutes on each side (a total
of 4–5 minutes).

Serve with a squeeze of fresh lime.

MAKES 24

eggplant dip with pomegranate seeds

2 tablespoons olive oil
1 garlic bulb
1 large eggplant (aubergine)
90 g (3¼ oz/⅓ cup) tahini
60 ml (2 fl oz/¼ cup) lemon juice
sea salt to taste
7 g (¼ oz/¼ cup) finely chopped flat-leaf (Italian) parsley
1 teaspoon sumac
seeds from 1 pomegranate

Preheat the oven to 220°C (425°F/Gas 7).

Put the olive oil into a small baking tin. Using a sharp knife halve the bulb of garlic from side to side so as to cut the cloves in half. Place the garlic halves cut side down onto the oiled pan and add the whole eggplant (aubergine). Place in a hot oven for approximately 20 minutes or until the cloves are golden brown and the eggplant is soft to the touch. Remove from oven and allow to cool.

With the tip of a small sharp knife remove the baked cloves from the garlic bulb and place them in a blender or food processor. Cut the eggplant in half, scoop out the soft flesh and add to the garlic. Blend. Remove to a bowl and fold in the tahini. Add the lemon juice and salt a little at a time, adjusting according to taste.

Just prior to serving, fold the chopped parsley through the dip. Garnish with a sprinkle of sumac and pomegranate seeds.

SERVES 4 AS AN ENTREE OR DIP

crab and celeriac remoulade on long toast

2 egg yolks
1 teaspoon Dijon mustard
juice of 1 lemon
150 ml (5 fl oz) light olive oil
½ celeriac, peeled and julienned
1 tablespoon finely chopped parsley
1 tablespoon snipped chives
150 g (5½ oz) fresh crabmeat
1 long red chilli, seeded and finely chopped
1 sourdough baguette
2 tablespoons extra virgin olive oil
½ teaspoon ground white pepper

Preheat the oven to 150°C (300°F/Gas 2).

Put the egg yolks, mustard and 1 tablespoon of lemon juice in a large bowl and whisk to combine. Slowly whisk in the light olive oil, a little at a time, until a thick mayonnaise forms.

Add the celeriac, parsley, chives, crabmeat and red chilli. Stir to combine, season to taste with sea salt and freshly ground black pepper, and add more lemon juice if necessary.

Slice the baguette in half lengthways, then thinly slice on an angle to make twelve toast fingers. Brush the extra virgin olive oil over the long pieces of bread, sprinkle with the white pepper and put them onto a tray and into the oven. Bake for a few minutes on each side until they are crisp and golden brown.

Arrange the toast on a serving platter and spoon the remoulade down the centre of each piece. Season with a little sea salt and freshly ground black pepper.

MAKES 12

salmon ceviche

500 g (1 lb 2 oz) salmon fillet
juice of 1 orange
juice and finely grated zest of 1 lime
juice of 1 lemon
¼ teaspoon ground white pepper
2 tablespoons finely chopped chives
4 large mint leaves, finely sliced
extra virgin olive oil, to serve

Finely dice the salmon and put it into a
ceramic bowl. Add the orange, lime and
lemon juice and the lime zest. Season with
a little ground white pepper and add the
chives and mint. Stir to combine. When
ready to serve, sprinkle with a little sea
salt and spoon into a serving dish.

Serve with thin toasts and
a drizzle of the extra
virgin olive oil.

SERVES 4

spiced sardines

½ red onion, finely sliced
1 garlic clove, finely chopped
2 tablespoons pine nuts
1 tablespoon currants
½ teaspoon ground coriander
2 tablespoons olive oil
12 fresh sardine fillets
juice and grated zest of 1 lemon
a handful of parsley leaves
2 tablespoons extra virgin olive oil,
to serve

Preheat the oven to 180°C (350°F/Gas 4).

Put the sliced onion, garlic, pine nuts, currants and ground coriander into the base of a small baking tin. Drizzle with the olive oil and bake for 10 minutes or until the onion is lightly caramelised. Remove from the oven and put the sardines over the mixture, skin side up. Bake for a further 15 minutes or until they are cooked through. Remove from the oven and cover with the lemon juice.

Remove the sardines to a ceramic serving plate and spoon the onion mixture and juices over them. Scatter with fresh parsley leaves and lemon zest and drizzle with extra virgin olive oil.

Serve with ciabatta toasts.

SERVES 4 AS AN ENTREE

chilli potatoes

500 g (1 lb 2 oz) potatoes
80 ml (2½ fl oz/⅓ cup) olive oil
½ teaspoon ground coriander
½ teaspoon ground cumin
1 teaspoon mustard seeds
½ teaspoon ground turmeric
1 red chilli, seeded and finely chopped

Peel the potatoes and cut them into small
bite-sized chunks.

Heat the olive oil in a heavy-based frying
pan over medium heat. Add the spices,
chilli and some sea salt to the oil. Stir once,
then add the potatoes to the oil and stir
them so that they are all well coated. Stir
the potatoes carefully around the pan
until they are soft and golden. When they
are cooked through, transfer them to a
serving bowl.

SERVES 4 AS NIBBLES

salt and pepper almonds

1 egg white
1 teaspoon soft brown sugar
1 teaspoon sea salt
¼ teaspoon smoky paprika
¼ teaspoon ground white pepper
200 g (7 oz) blanched almonds

Preheat the oven to 180°C (350°F/Gas 4).

Line a baking tray with baking paper.

Put the egg white into a bowl and whisk until it is frothy. Add the brown sugar, sea salt, paprika and pepper and whisk to combine. Toss the almonds in the flavoured egg white and, with a slotted spoon, remove them to the baking tray.

Bake the almonds in the oven for 10 minutes or until they are golden brown. Remove and allow to cool before storing in an airtight container.

You may wish to add a little more sea salt to the almonds at this stage.

SERVES 4 AS NIBBLES

citrus-scented olives and caperberries

500 g (1 lb 2 oz) mixed olives
zest and juice of 1 orange
zest and juice of 1 lemon
1 garlic clove, crushed
4 sprigs thyme
100 g (3½ oz) caperberries, drained
    and sliced in half lengthways
100 ml (3½ fl oz) extra virgin olive oil

Put the olives, orange zest and juice, lemon zest and juice, garlic, thyme and caperberries into a bowl and toss to combine. Drizzle with the extra virgin olive oil and allow to marinate for at least an hour or, preferably, overnight before serving.

SERVES 4 AS NIBBLES

piquant buffalo mozzarella bites

30 g (1 oz/¼ cup) finely chopped semi-dried tomatoes
2 tablespoons small salted capers, rinsed and finely chopped
2 tablespoons finely chopped parsley
4 large green olives, finely chopped
1 teaspoon orange zest, finely chopped
2 buffalo mozzarella cheeses
extra virgin olive oil, to serve

In a small bowl combine the chopped tomatoes, capers, parsley, olives and orange zest and toss to distribute the ingredients evenly.

Tear the cheeses into small bite-sized pieces and arrange on a serving plate. Spoon the tomato mixture over the pieces of mozzarella and season with freshly ground black pepper. Drizzle with the extra virgin olive oil and serve.

SERVES 4 AS A SIDE DISH

zen

calming bowls of goodness

STEAMED GREENS WITH ARAME AND SESAME SALT
GREEN BROTH
BAKED BLUE EYE COD WITH HERB SALAD
STEAMED FISH WITH CHILLI CARAMEL
GREEN TEA NOODLES WITH ASPARAGUS AND MUSHROOMS
CRAB AND WATERCRESS SOUP
MISO AND CHICKEN SOUP WITH TOFU
STEAMED EGGPLANT WITH TOFU, GINGER
AND SPRING ONION
MARINATED OCEAN TROUT WITH BUCKWHEAT NOODLES
PRAWN AND LEMONGRASS SOUP

steamed greens with arame and sesame salt

50 g (1¾ oz/⅓ cup) sesame seeds
2 teaspoons sea salt
2 heaped tablespoons dried arame
4 baby bok choy, halved
100 g (3½ oz) small green beans, trimmed
100 g (3½ oz) broccoli florets

Put the sesame seeds into a small saucepan over low heat and cook until the seeds are lightly golden. Remove from the pan and put into a mortar and pestle or spice grinder with the sea salt. Grind the sesame seeds and salt together, then remove them to a small serving bowl.

Put the arame into a small bowl and cover with boiling water. Allow to steep for 10 minutes, then drain and set aside.

Fill a large, wide saucepan with water to a depth of 6 cm (2½ in) and bring the water to the boil. Rest the base of a bamboo steamer basket in the boiling water. Put the baby bok choy into a second steamer basket on top of the first, cover, and steam for 2 minutes. Put the beans and broccoli into a third basket and place it on top of the bok choy. Cover, and steam for a further 4 minutes.

Arrange the steamed greens on a serving plate. Sprinkle with some of the sesame salt and scatter with the arame.

SERVES 4 AS A SIDE DISH

green broth

2 tablespoons olive oil
2 garlic cloves, crushed
1 leek, rinsed and diced
4 shallots, peeled and chopped
500 g (1 lb 2 oz) baby peas
1 litre (35 fl oz/4 cups) vegetable or
　　chicken stock
100 g (3½ oz) baby spinach leaves
60 g (2¼ oz/1 cup, packed) cavolo
　　nero leaves
12 mint leaves
7 g (¼ oz/⅓ cup) picked chervil leaves,
　　plus extra for garnish
7 g (¼ oz/⅓ cup) picked parsley
　　leaves, plus extra for garnish
juice and zest of 1 lemon

Heat the olive oil in a large saucepan
over medium heat, then add the garlic,
leek and shallots and cook until soft and
lightly golden. Add the peas and stock,
cook for 6 minutes, then add the leaves,
herbs and lemon juice. Once all the leaves
and herbs have wilted, remove the broth
from the heat and purée in a blender or
food processor until smooth. Season to
taste with sea salt and freshly ground
black pepper.

To serve, ladle into four warm bowls and
garnish with little bouquets of herbs and
lemon zest threads.

SERVES 4

baked blue eye cod with herb salad

8 spring onions (scallions)
1 tablespoon olive oil
1 teaspoon red chilli flakes
4 x 185 g (6½ oz) blue eye cod fillets
1½ teaspoons finely grated lemon zest
20 g (¾ oz) butter
60 ml (2 fl oz/¼ cup) orange juice
2 tablespoons walnut oil
1½ teaspoons lemon juice
30 g (1 oz/½ cup) dill, coarsely chopped
10 g (¼ oz/½ cup) flat-leaf (Italian) parsley leaves, coarsely chopped
7 g (¼ oz/⅓ cup) mint leaves, finely chopped
20 g (¾ oz/⅓ cup) chives, snipped

Preheat the oven to 200°C (400°F/Gas 6).

Cut the spring onions into 5 cm (2 in) lengths and slice them lengthways. Heat the olive oil in a non-stick frying pan and cook the spring onions and chilli flakes until the spring onions are soft and beginning to colour.

Rinse the fish fillets under cold running water and pat dry with paper towel. Put the fish fillets into a baking tin and cover with the cooked spring onions and lemon zest. Dot each piece of fish with the butter and pour the orange juice into the dish. Cover and bake in the oven for 15 minutes.

Put the walnut oil and lemon juice into a bowl and whisk to combine.

Put the fish onto four serving plates and spoon some of the juices over. Top with the mixed herbs and drizzle with the walnut and lemon dressing.

SERVES 4

steamed fish with chilli caramel

chilli caramel
2 red chillies, seeded and finely chopped
1 tablespoon finely chopped lemongrass
1 tablespoon olive oil
1 tablespoon caster (superfine) sugar
2 tablespoons white wine vinegar
1 teaspoon soy sauce

4 x 150 g (5½ oz) snapper fillets
200 g (7 oz) peeled and finely julienned daikon
½ red capsicum (pepper), finely julienned
100 g (3½ oz) snow peas (mangetout), trimmed and finely julienned
2 limes, halved, to serve

Make the chilli caramel in a small saucepan by sweating the chillies and lemongrass in the olive oil over low heat, then adding the sugar, vinegar and 1 tablespoon of water. Cook until it turns into a syrup, then add the soy sauce. Allow to cool.

Fill a large, wide saucepan with water to a depth of 6 cm (2½ in) and bring the water to the boil.

Rinse the fish fillets under cold running water and pat dry with paper towel.

Rest the base of a bamboo steamer in the boiling water. Line a second bamboo steaming basket with a square of baking paper, sit the fish fillets on the paper and sprinkle with a little sea salt. Cover the basket, then sit it on top of the bamboo steamer base and steam the fish for 7–8 minutes, depending on the thickness of the fillets.

Meanwhile, toss the daikon, red capsicum (pepper) and snow peas together in a large bowl.

Put the steamed fish on four warm serving plates and drizzle with the chilli caramel. Serve with the salad and some fresh lime.

SERVES 4

green tea noodles with asparagus and mushrooms

10 dried shiitake mushrooms
300 g (10½ oz) green tea noodles
2 bunches of asparagus
6 spring onions (scallions)
1 tablespoon sesame oil
2 tablespoons sunflower oil
1 large red chilli, seeded and thinly sliced
3 cm (1¼ in) piece ginger, peeled and thinly sliced
100 g (3½ oz) oyster mushrooms
50 g (1¾ oz) enoki mushrooms, trimmed
2 large garlic cloves, thinly sliced
60 ml (2 fl oz/¼ cup) tamari

Put the shiitake mushrooms in a bowl and cover with boiling water. Allow to sit for 10 minutes or until soft. Drain the mushrooms and thinly slice them.

Cook the noodles in a large pot of boiling salted water for 2 minutes, drain and refresh in cold water. Divide among four bowls.

Trim the asparagus ends and slice each spear into thirds on the diagonal. Cut the spring onions into 4 cm (1½ in) lengths.

Put the oils into a wok or large frying pan and heat over medium heat. Add the chilli and ginger to the wok and cook until they begin to colour. Increase the heat to high, add the vegetables and garlic, and stir to cook evenly. Continue to cook until the asparagus is glossy and has turned a deep green. Add the tamari and cook for a further minute.

Divide the vegetables among the four bowls and serve immediately.

SERVES 4

crab and watercress soup

2 corn cobs
1 leek (white part only)
40 g (1½ oz) butter
1.5 litres (52 fl oz/6 cups)
chicken stock
200 g (7 oz) cooked crabmeat
2 handfuls of watercress sprigs
1 spring onion (scallion), finely sliced

Using a sharp knife cut the corn kernels away from the cobs. Slice the leek in half lengthways and rinse. Dry with paper towel and then slice in half lengthways again. Finely slice the leek quarters. Put them into a large saucepan with the corn and the butter. Heat over medium to high heat until the leek is soft and the corn has turned golden yellow. Add the chicken stock and bring to the boil. Add the crabmeat and reduce to a simmer. Simmer for 10 minutes.

Ladle the soup into four warm bowls. Add the watercress, sprinkle with the spring onion and serve.

SERVES 4

miso and chicken soup with tofu

1.5 litres (52 fl oz/6 cups) chicken
   stock
1 teaspoon finely grated ginger
2 spring onions (scallions), finely
   sliced
2 chicken breasts, thinly sliced
80 ml (2½ fl oz/⅓ cup) miso paste
500 g (1 lb 2 oz) firm tofu, cubed
100 g (3½ oz) snow peas (mangetout),
   julienned

Put the stock, ginger and shallots into a
large saucepan over high heat and bring to
the boil. Reduce the heat and simmer for
15 minutes, then remove 250 ml (9 fl oz/
1 cup) of the stock. Add the chicken slices
to the saucepan.

Put the removed broth into a bowl and add
the miso. Stir to combine.

Add the tofu and snow peas (mangetout)
to the saucepan and bring the soup to the
boil one more time. Remove from the heat,
add the miso and stir it through.

Ladle the soup into four warmed bowls
and serve.

SERVES 4

steamed eggplant with tofu, ginger and spring onion

1 large eggplant (aubergine)
2 tablespoons shao hsing wine
1 teaspoon soft brown sugar
2 tablespoons light soy sauce
¼ teaspoon sesame oil
300 g (10½ oz) silken tofu, cut into chunks
2 spring onions (scallions), finely sliced
4 cm (1½ in) piece ginger, peeled and julienned
2 tablespoons peanut oil

Cut the eggplant (aubergine) in half lengthways, then cut the halves into long strips approximately 1 cm (½ in) wide. Put the eggplant strips onto a clean tray and sprinkle with a little salt. Allow them to sit for 10 minutes.

Fill a large, wide saucepan with water to a depth of 6 cm (2½ in) and bring the water to the boil. Rest the base of a bamboo steaming basket in the boiling water.

Rinse the eggplant strips under cold running water, pat them dry with paper towel, then put them on a heatproof plate. Place the plate inside the steamer, cover, and steam for 8 minutes.

In a small bowl combine the shao hsing wine, brown sugar, light soy sauce and sesame oil. Stir until the sugar has dissolved, then set aside.

Arrange the steamed eggplant on a serving platter, then put the tofu on top. Scatter the spring onion and ginger over the tofu, and spoon the dressing over.

Heat the peanut oil in a small frying pan until hot, then pour it over the spring onion and ginger.

Serve with steamed rice and seared fish or chicken.

SERVES 4 AS A SIDE DISH

marinated ocean trout with buckwheat noodles

500 g (1 lb 2 oz) ocean trout fillet, skin and bones removed
1 tablespoon sesame oil
4 spring onions (scallions), trimmed and cut into 3 cm (1¼ in) lengths
185 ml (6 fl oz/¾ cup) rice wine vinegar
55 g (2 oz/¼ cup) sugar
2 cm (¾ in) piece ginger, peeled and julienned
1 small red chilli, sliced in half
10 cm (4 in) piece lemongrass stem, finely chopped
2 star anise
1 teaspoon sichuan peppercorns
300 g (10½ oz) buckwheat noodles
1 Lebanese (short) cucumber, diced
1 red capsicum (pepper), julienned
1 lime, quartered

Cut the fish into 1 cm (½ in) wide slices and put them in a single layer in a large, deep non-metallic dish.

Put the sesame oil and the spring onions in a saucepan over medium heat and cook until the spring onions have softened and are starting to turn golden brown. Pour 375 ml (13 fl oz/1½ cups) of water over the spring onions and add the vinegar, sugar, ginger, chilli, lemongrass, star anise and sichuan peppercorns. Bring to the boil, stirring to dissolve the sugar, then pour the hot liquid over the ocean trout and leave it to cool.

Cook the buckwheat noodles until *al dente*, then drain and rinse. Divide the noodles among four bowls and top with the marinated trout, cucumber and capsicum. Drizzle with some of the marinating liquid and serve with a squeeze of fresh lime.

SERVES 4

prawn and lemongrass soup

12 green king prawns
3 lemongrass stems
100 g (3½ oz) oyster mushrooms
100 g (3½ oz) enoki mushrooms
6 kaffir lime leaves
2 spring onions (scallions), finely sliced
150 g (5½ oz) bean sprouts
juice of 3 limes
2 small red chillies, finely sliced
80 ml (2½ fl oz/⅓ cup) fish sauce
coriander (cilantro) and mint leaves, to garnish

Peel and devein the prawns and set aside the shells. Cut the white part off the lemongrass stems, reserving the tops. Cut the white lemongrass stems into 2 cm (½ in) lengths and flatten with a cleaver or the end of a heavy-handled knife or rolling pin.

Heat 1 litre (35 fl oz/4 cups) of water in a saucepan over high heat, then add the prawn shells and the lemongrass tops. Bring the water to the boil, simmer for 10 minutes, then strain into a large bowl and return the prawn stock to the saucepan. Add the crushed lemongrass, the mushrooms and the kaffir lime leaves. Return to the boil, then reduce the heat and simmer for 3–4 minutes. Add the prawns and as they start to turn pink, add the spring onion, bean sprouts, lime juice, chilli and fish sauce. Stir well, then season to taste with sea salt and freshly ground black pepper.

Ladle into four warmed bowls and serve with a sprinkle of coriander (cilantro) and mint.

SERVES 4

tang

tastes of savoury citrus and zest

AVOCADO AND SMOKED SALMON SALAD
BAKED VEGETABLE TART WITH LEMON CREME
LEMON AND LIME ROAST CHICKEN
PAN-FRIED BREAM WITH CUMIN AND LEMON SALT
SQUID SALAD
CHICKEN SATAY SALAD
BAKED CHICKEN BREAST WITH A PRESERVED LEMON DRESSING
SOUPY MUSSELS
COCONUT FISH CURRY
SICHUAN PORK WITH AN ORANGE FENNEL SALAD

avocado and smoked salmon salad

2 tablespoons currants
80 ml (2½ fl oz/⅓ cup) boiling water
1 tablespoon baby capers
2 teaspoons finely grated lemon zest
1 tablespoon lemon juice
60 ml (2 fl oz/¼ cup) extra virgin olive oil
2 avocados
2 zucchini (courgettes)
12 slices smoked salmon
1 bunch watercress, sprigs picked

Put the currants into a small bowl and cover with the boiling water.
Allow to sit for 5 minutes, then drain.

Put the currants into a small bowl with the capers, lemon zest, lemon
juice and extra virgin olive oil.

Halve the avocados, remove the stones and dice the flesh. Add the
diced avocado to the dressing.

Trim the top and bottom of the zucchini (courgettes) and thinly slice
them into long strips, using a vegetable peeler.

Divide the smoked salmon among four plates and arrange the
watercress and zucchini strips on top. Spoon the dressed avocado
over the salad.

SERVES 4

baked vegetable tart with lemon creme

500 g (1 lb 2 oz) sweet potato, peeled
2 medium beetroot (beets), peeled
150 g (5½ oz) shallots, peeled and halved
6 sprigs thyme
80 ml (2½ fl oz/⅓ cup) extra virgin olive oil
1 teaspoon sumac
1 red capsicum (pepper)
1½ sheets frozen puff pastry, thawed
200 g (7 oz) light sour cream
1 tablespoon lemon juice
lemon wedges and basil leaves, to serve

Preheat the oven to 180°C (350°F/Gas 4).

Line a roasting tin and a baking tray with baking paper.

Cut the sweet potato and beetroot (beets) into 2 cm (¾ in) square chunks and put them into a bowl with the shallots, thyme, extra virgin olive oil and sumac. Season with sea salt and toss several times to ensure that the vegetables are well coated in the spiced oil, then put them into the roasting tin. Bake in the oven for 30 minutes. Add the diced red capsicum (pepper) and bake for a further 15 minutes, then remove from the oven.

Lay the sheets of puff pastry onto the lined baking tray, slightly moistening the end of each sheet to join them where they overlap. Roll 1 cm (½ in) of pastry over on all sides to form an edge. Arrange the baked vegetables over the pastry and bake for 30 minutes or until the pastry is puffed and golden.

In a small bowl combine the sour cream and lemon juice. Stir until smooth and season with a little freshly ground black pepper.

Cut the tart into squares, drizzle with the lemon cream, and serve with lemon wedges and a scattering of basil leaves.

SERVES 4–6

lemon and lime roast chicken

2 lime leaves, sliced
1 lemongrass stem, trimmed and
    roughly chopped
3 garlic cloves
2 cm (¾ in) ginger, peeled and chopped
2 red chillies, seeded and chopped
2 tablespoons extra virgin olive oil
1 whole chicken
1 lime, halved

Preheat the oven to 180°C (350°F/Gas 4).

Put the lime leaves, lemongrass, garlic, ginger, chillies and extra virgin olive oil into a food processor and blend to a paste.

Rinse the chicken under cold running water and pat dry with paper towel. Using your fingers make a small pocket under the skin at the breast and insert half the seasoning. Rub the remaining seasoning inside the chicken and all over the skin. Put the chicken in a shallow roasting tin and roast for 1½ hours.

Remove from the oven, squeeze the fresh lime over the chicken, then return to the oven for a further 5 minutes. Remove, cover with foil and allow to rest for 10 minutes. Carve into serving pieces and drizzle with pan juices. Serve with steamed rice and greens.

SERVES 6

pan-fried bream with cumin and lemon salt

1 teaspoon cumin seeds
1 tablespoon sea salt
juice and finely grated zest of 1 lemon
4 x 180 g (6¼ oz) bream fillets
40 g (1½ oz) butter
leafy green salad, to serve

Heat a small frying pan over high heat and add the cumin seeds. Fry the seeds until they are aromatic and starting to darken, then remove them to a mortar and pestle. Add the sea salt and finely grated lemon zest, and grind the ingredients until they are well combined. Set aside.

Rinse the fish fillets under cold running water and pat dry with paper towel.

Heat a large frying pan over high heat and add the butter. When the butter is sizzling put the fillets into the pan, skin side down, and fry for 5 minutes. Flip the fillets over, drizzle with the lemon juice and cook for a further 5 minutes or until the fillets are cooked through. Serve the bream with a leafy green salad, a sprinkle of the flavoured salt and some grated lemon zest.

SERVES 4

squid salad

10 small squid, about 1 kg (2 lb 4 oz), cleaned
1 tablespoon caster (superfine) sugar
2 tablespoons lime juice
½ teaspoon finely grated lime zest
1 tablespoon fish sauce
2 tablespoons peanut oil
2 garlic cloves, finely chopped
3 vine-ripened tomatoes, roughly chopped
1 Lebanese (short) cucumber, roughly chopped
1 small red onion, finely sliced
2 large red chillies, seeded and finely chopped
a handful of fresh mint leaves
a handful of fresh coriander (cilantro) leaves

Rinse the cleaned squid under cold running water and pat dry with paper towel. Remove the tentacles and set them aside. Cut the tubes along one side and open each one out into a flat piece. Using a sharp knife, lightly score the inside surface with crisscross lines to make the squid curl up during cooking—don't cut too deeply, just enough to mark the flesh. Slice into 3 cm (1¼ in) wide strips and put the strips and tentacles in a bowl.

In a large bowl, combine the sugar with the lime juice, lime zest and fish sauce. Stir until the sugar dissolves.

Warm the peanut oil and garlic over high heat and, before the garlic begins to colour, add the squid pieces in batches and cook for 5 minutes or until tender. Add the batches of cooked squid to the bowl with the dressing, and toss to ensure all pieces of squid are well coated.

Add the tomato, cucumber, onion and chilli. Toss to combine, then allow the salad to sit for 10 minutes. Serve with steamed rice and a scattering of fresh herbs.

SERVES 4

chicken satay salad

1 tablespoon palm sugar (jaggery)
80 ml (2½ fl oz/⅓ cup) boiling water
½ tablespoon balsamic vinegar
1 tablespoon kecap manis
2 garlic cloves, finely chopped
1 red chilli, seeded and finely chopped
80 g (2¾ oz/½ cup) roasted and ground peanuts

4 chicken breasts
3 limes, quartered
100 g (3½ oz) baby leaf salad
2 Lebanese (short) cucumbers, cut into chunks
2 handfuls bean sprouts

In a small bowl, combine the palm sugar (jaggery), boiling water, vinegar and kecap manis. Stir well until the palm sugar has dissolved. Add the garlic, red chilli and ground peanuts and stir to combine. Set aside.

Cut each chicken breast into four lengthways. Heat a ridged grill plate or heavy-based frying pan over high heat and cook the chicken strips for 2 minutes on each side.

Remove the chicken from the heat to a clean plate and squeeze the juice from one of the limes over the chicken.

Divide the baby leaf salad among four serving plates and top with the cucumber and bean sprouts. Arrange the chicken over the top and serve with the satay sauce and the remaining lime quarters.

SERVES 4

baked chicken breast
with a preserved lemon dressing

4 boneless chicken breasts, skin on
20 mint leaves, roughly chopped
2 handfuls flat-leaf (Italian) parsley leaves, roughly chopped
2 tablespoons finely chopped preserved lemon rind
125 ml (4 fl oz/½ cup) extra virgin olive oil
2 tablespoons lemon juice
1 Lebanese (short) cucumber, diced
1 tablespoon soft goat's cheese

Preheat the oven to 180°C (350°F/Gas 4).

Heat a non-stick frying pan over high heat and cook the chicken
breasts for a few minutes, skin side down, until the skin is golden
and crispy. Remove the breasts to a roasting tray and cook in the
oven, skin side up, for a further 15 minutes or until the chicken is
cooked through.

Meanwhile, put the mint, parsley, preserved lemon, extra virgin olive
oil, lemon juice and cucumber into a bowl and combine.

Remove the chicken from the oven and put onto four serving plates.
Spoon the herb salad over the chicken breasts and top each one with
a teaspoonful of the goat's cheese. Serve with roast potatoes.

SERVES 4

soupy mussels

1 kg (2 lb 4 oz) mussels
1 tablespoon olive oil
1 leek, rinsed and finely chopped
2 garlic cloves, finely chopped
¼ teaspoon cayenne pepper
½ teaspoon ground cumin
1 tablespoon finely grated fresh ginger
400 g (14 oz) tin chopped tomatoes
200 ml (7 fl oz) coconut cream
a handful of coriander (cilantro) leaves

Rinse and scrub the mussels. Discard any that remain open.

Warm the olive oil in a large frying pan over medium heat and cook the leek and garlic until soft and golden brown. Add the cayenne pepper, cumin and ginger. Cook for a further minute before adding the tomatoes. Bring to the boil, then add the mussels. Cover and steam for 8–10 minutes or until all the mussels have opened.

Remove the mussels from the pan and divide them among four warm bowls. Add 200 ml (7 fl oz) of water to the pan and return to the boil.

Once the soupy mixture has boiled remove the pan from the heat, stir in the coconut cream and ladle the mixture over the mussels. Serve with a scatter of coriander (cilantro) leaves.

SERVES 4

coconut fish curry

400 g (14 oz) waxy potatoes, peeled and cut into chunks
80 ml (2½ fl oz/⅓ cup) olive oil
1 large red onion, finely chopped
20 saffron threads
½ teaspoon chilli flakes
1 teaspoon ground cumin
2 celery stalks, sliced
1 small cinnamon stick
400 g (14 oz) tin chopped tomatoes
400 ml (14 fl oz) coconut milk
600 g (1 lb 5 oz) ling fillets, cut into chunks
a handful of coriander (cilantro) leaves
2 tablespoons finely chopped preserved lemon rind

Put the potato chunks into a saucepan and cover with cold water.
Bring to the boil and cook for 15 minutes. Drain and set aside.

Heat the olive oil in a large saucepan or casserole pot over medium
heat. Add the onion, saffron, chilli flakes and cumin and cook until
the onion is soft and slightly caramelised. Add the potatoes, celery,
cinnamon stick, tomatoes and coconut milk. Simmer for 10 minutes.
Season the fish chunks with sea salt and add them to the curry.
Simmer for a further 10 minutes, then season with freshly ground
black pepper.

Garnish with the coriander (cilantro) leaves and preserved lemon
and serve with steamed rice or a mixed leaf salad.

SERVES 4

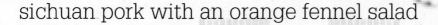

sichuan pork with an orange fennel salad

2 fennel bulbs, trimmed and thinly sliced
4 blood oranges, peeled and thinly sliced
2 teaspoons sea salt
2 teaspoons sichuan peppercorns
1 teaspoon white peppercorns
4 x 150 g (5½ oz) pork steaks, flattened schnitzel style
2 teaspoons olive oil, for frying
40 g (1½ oz/2 cups) picked chervil
80 ml (2½ fl oz/⅓ cup) extra virgin olive oil

Put the fennel and orange in a bowl with 1 teaspoon of the sea salt. Set aside.

Pulse the sichuan peppercorns, white peppercorns and the remaining teaspoon of sea salt in a spice grinder, or crush with a mortar and pestle. Pour the spices onto a plate and press the pork steaks into them, making sure each steak is well coated.

Heat the olive oil in a non-stick frying pan over medium heat. When the oil begins to shimmer, put the seasoned steaks into the pan and cook for 4–5 minutes on each side. Remove from heat, allow to rest for 5 minutes, then cut into thick slices.

Toss the chervil through the fennel and orange salad, dress with the extra virgin olive oil and layer on four serving plates with the spiced pork slices.

SERVES 4

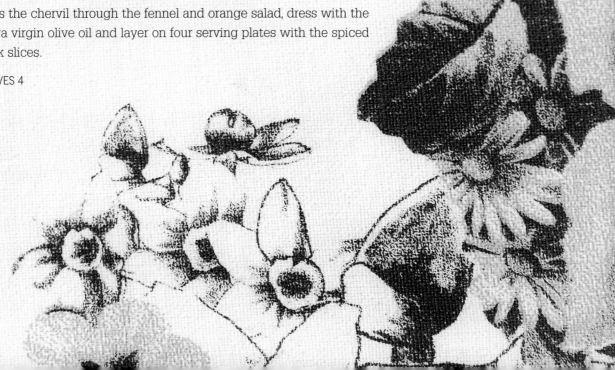

earthy

warming spices, rich flavours

PUMPKIN DHAL
ROAST SESAME AND BEETROOT SALAD
PEAR AND WALNUT SALAD
SAFFRON RICE WITH GARLIC PRAWNS
CHICKEN MEATBALL SALAD
CHERMOULA FISH
PORTUGUESE LAMB
BEEF AND POTATO CURRY
CHICKEN AND BABY FIG TAGINE
CUMIN-CRUSTED LAMB RACK

pumpkin dhal

300 g (10½ oz) yellow split peas
1 teaspoon brown sugar
1 teaspoon ground turmeric
2 cm (½ in) piece ginger, peeled and finely grated
½ teaspoon ground cumin
300 g (10½ oz) pumpkin (winter squash), diced
juice of 1 lime
2 tablespoons olive oil
1 teaspoon black mustard seeds
2 garlic cloves, finely chopped
1 long red chilli, sliced into thin circles

Rinse the split peas, then cover with water and allow to soak for an hour. Drain.

Put 1.5 litres (52 fl oz/6 cups) of water in a large saucepan and bring to the boil. Add the drained split peas, the sugar, turmeric, ginger, cumin and pumpkin. Boil for 30 minutes. Remove from the heat and stir the lime juice through.

In a small frying pan heat the oil over high heat and fry the mustard seeds for 3–4 minutes or until the mustard seeds pop, then add the garlic and chilli.

Put the dhal into a serving dish and spoon the spice mix over.

SERVES 4

roast sesame and beetroot salad

50 g (1¾ oz/⅓ cup) sesame seeds
1 tablespoon ground coriander
4 medium beetroot (beets)
80 ml (2½ fl oz/⅓ cup) balsamic
    vinegar
80 ml (2½ fl oz/⅓ cup) extra virgin
    olive oil
a handful of mint leaves, roughly
    chopped

Put the sesame seeds and ground coriander into a small frying pan and dry toast them over medium heat until the sesame seeds are lightly golden. Set aside.

Wearing rubber gloves, peel the beetroots and grate them into a bowl. Add the toasted sesame seeds and coriander with the vinegar and extra virgin olive oil and stir to combine. Season to taste with sea salt and freshly ground black pepper.

Spoon the beetroot into a serving dish and scatter with the mint leaves.

SERVES 4 AS A SIDE DISH

pear and walnut salad

100 g (3½ oz/1 cup) walnut halves
½ garlic clove
1 teaspoon sea salt
juice and grated zest of 1 orange
125 ml (4 fl oz/½ cup) light olive oil
4 beurre bosc pears, thinly sliced
100 g (3½ oz) lambs lettuce
140 g (5 oz) goat's curd

Put the walnuts, garlic, sea salt, grated orange zest and olive oil in a blender or food processor and process to form a thick sauce.

Put the orange juice into a bowl and add the sliced pear. Season with some freshly ground black pepper. Add the lambs lettuce and toss lightly to combine.

Divide the salad among four serving plates and spoon the goat's curd on top. Drizzle the salad with any remaining orange juice, then spoon the walnut dressing over the goat's curd.

SERVES 4

saffron rice with garlic prawns

¼ teaspoon saffron threads
200 g (7 oz/1 cup) basmati rice
1 punnet cherry tomatoes
2 tablespoons olive oil
2 onions, peeled and diced
3 whole cloves
300 ml (10½ fl oz) chicken stock
40 g (1½ oz) butter
3 garlic cloves, crushed
20 green king prawns, peeled and deveined
a handful of coriander (cilantro) leaves

Put the saffron threads in a small bowl with 1 tablespoon of hot water.

Rinse the rice several times, then put in a bowl and cover with water.

Cut the cherry tomatoes in half. Squeeze out the seeds and discard them.

Put a large heavy-based saucepan over medium heat and add the olive oil, onion and cloves. Cook until the onion is soft. Drain the rice and add it to the saucepan along with the chicken stock and the saffron mix. Season with some sea salt. Bring to the boil, stirring to ensure that the rice does not settle. Reduce the heat to medium and simmer, partially covered, for 10 minutes or until most of the liquid has been absorbed. Remove from the heat and cover tightly. Allow to sit for 10 minutes.

Heat the butter in a heavy-based frying pan and add the garlic. When the butter is sizzling add the prawns a few at a time and cook for a few minutes on each side, removing to a warm plate as they are done. When all the prawns have been cooked, add the tomatoes to the garlicky butter, season with a little sea salt and cook until soft.

Spoon the rice into four bowls and top with the coriander (cilantro) and prawns. Add the cooked tomatoes and drizzle with the garlicky juices.

SERVES 4

chicken meatball salad

500 g (1 lb 2 oz) minced (ground)
    chicken
4 spring onions (scallions), finely
    sliced
25 g (1 oz/½ cup) chopped coriander
    (cilantro) leaves
1½ teaspoons sea salt
1½ tablespoons sesame seeds
1 teaspoon chilli flakes
finely grated zest of 3 oranges
¾ teaspoon ground white pepper
mixed leaf salad, to serve
tahini dressing, to serve (see extras,
    page 244)

Preheat the oven to 180°C (350°F/Gas 4).

Line a baking tray with baking paper.

Put the chicken, spring onions (scallions),
coriander (cilantro) leaves and 1 teaspoon of
the sea salt into a bowl and combine well.

Put the sesame seeds, chilli flakes, orange
zest, white pepper and remaining sea salt
into a large pasta bowl and stir to combine.

Roll the chicken mixture into walnut-sized
balls, then roll them in the spice mix. Put
them onto the prepared tray. Bake in the
oven for 20–25 minutes or until cooked
through and golden brown.

Remove and serve with the mixed leaf
salad and a dollop of tahini dressing.

SERVES 4

chermoula fish

1 tablespoon cumin seeds
1 tablespoon coriander seeds
1 tablespoon paprika
1 tablespoon grated fresh ginger
2 garlic cloves
1 roasted red capsicum (pepper),
    seeded and skin removed
20 g (¾ cup) roughly chopped
    coriander (cilantro) leaves
2 tablespoons olive oil
4 x 200 g (7 oz) kingfish fillets, skin
    left on
lemon wedges, to serve
green salad, to serve

Preheat the oven to 200°C (400°F/Gas 6).

Put all the ingredients except the fish into
a food processor and process to a thick
paste. Season to taste with sea salt and
freshly ground black pepper.

Rub the paste over the fish fillets. Put the
fish, skin side up, on a baking tray and
season with sea salt. Bake for 12 minutes.
Remove from the oven and use the point of
a small knife to check that the fish is
cooked through.

Put the fish fillets onto four plates and
garnish with lemon wedges. Serve with
a green salad.

SERVES 4

portuguese lamb

1 shoulder of lamb
6 garlic cloves, crushed
10 cardamom pods, crushed
250 ml (9 fl oz/1 cup) red wine
zest and juice of 2 lemons
125 ml (4 fl oz/½ cup) extra virgin olive oil
steamed green beans and mashed potato, to serve

With a sharp knife, cut slits in the lamb and insert garlic into the flesh, then put the lamb in a non-metallic dish.

Mix the remaining ingredients together and drizzle over the lamb. Cover and refrigerate, allowing the meat to marinate for at least 4 hours.

Preheat the oven to 150°C (300°F/Gas 2).

Put the lamb and the marinade into a roasting tin and roast in the oven for 1 hour. Remove, baste with the juice, cover with foil and cook for a further 40 minutes.

Remove from the oven and allow to rest, covered, for 15 minutes. Slice the lamb and serve with some baking juices, steamed green beans and mashed potato.

SERVES 4

beef and potato curry

350 g (12 oz) waxy potatoes, peeled and cubed
1 teaspoon ground turmeric
2 tablespoons olive oil
2 tablespoons grated fresh ginger
1 tablespoon ground coriander
2 teaspoons mustard seeds
1 teaspoon fennel seeds
1 teaspoon dried red chilli
2 onions, sliced
750 g (1 lb 10 oz) diced beef
6 green chillies, seeded and cut into long thin strips
1 tablespoon tomato paste (concentrated purée)
400 g (14 oz) tin chopped tomatoes
steamed rice or couscous, to serve

Put the potatoes in a large saucepan and cover with water. Add the powder and 1 teaspoon of sea salt and bring to the boil over high heat. Reduce the heat to low, cover and cook for 15 minutes or until the potatoes are cooked through. Drain and set aside, reserving some of the liquid to add to the curry later.

Put a heavy-based frying pan over medium heat and add 1 tablespoon of olive oil and the ginger, coriander, mustard seeds, fennel seeds and chilli. Cook for a minute or until the spices are aromatic, then add the onion and the remaining olive oil. Cook the onion until it is soft, then remove it with a slotted spoon. Add the beef to the pan and cook, stirring occasionally, until the meat is browned. Return the spiced onions to the pan, and add the green chilli, tomato paste and tomatoes.

Reduce the heat to low, cover, and allow to simmer for 30 minutes, adding some of the reserved potato water if necessary.

Add the potatoes at the last minute and cook for a further minute.

Serve with steamed rice or couscous.

SERVES 4

chicken and baby fig tagine

60 ml (2 fl oz/¼ cup) extra virgin olive oil
2 onions, diced
2 garlic cloves, crushed
2 teaspoons finely grated fresh ginger
10 saffron threads
1 teaspoon freshly ground black pepper
1 kg (2 lb 4 oz) roughly chopped chicken thigh meat
500 ml (17 fl oz/2 cups) chicken stock
120 g (4¼ oz) dried baby figs
100 g (3½ oz) dates
2 bay leaves
1 cinnamon stick
20 g (¾ oz/⅓ cup) chopped parsley leaves
2 tablespoons lemon juice

Put the extra virgin olive oil in a large saucepan over medium heat and add the onion, garlic, ginger, saffron and black pepper. Stir to combine, and cook for several minutes or until the onion is soft and golden brown.

Add the chopped chicken and cook until the chicken is lightly golden all over, then add the stock, figs, dates, bay leaves and cinnamon stick. Bring to the boil, then reduce the heat and cook gently for 30 minutes.

Season to taste with sea salt and freshly ground black pepper, then add the parsley and lemon juice.

Serve with steamed couscous.

SERVES 4

cumin-crusted lamb rack

4 small racks of lamb, consisting of 3–4 cutlets each
55 g (2 oz/½ cup) ground almonds
2 tablespoons sesame seeds
2 tablespoons chopped parsley
2 tablespoons ground cumin
2 garlic cloves, finely chopped
1 tablespoon olive oil
400 g (14 oz) tin white beans, drained
1 punnet cherry tomatoes, halved
a handful of flat-leaf (Italian) parsley, roughly chopped
1 tablespoon salted capers, rinsed
2 tablespoons extra virgin olive oil
2 teaspoons balsamic vinegar

Preheat the oven to 200°C (400°F/Gas 6).

Trim the lamb racks, removing any excess fat.

Mix the almond meal, sesame seeds, parsley, cumin, garlic and olive oil in a small bowl and season with 1 teaspoon of sea salt and some freshly ground black pepper. Put the mixture onto the face of each rack of lamb and press on firmly to make a crust.

Put the lamb racks in a roasting tin and roast in the oven for 20–25 minutes, remove and allow to rest for 5 minutes.

In a large bowl combine the beans, tomatoes, parsley, capers, extra virgin olive oil and the vinegar. Toss to combine, and season with freshly ground black pepper.

Serve the racks with the white bean salad.

SERVES 4

warmth

hearty food for wintry days

RED LENTIL, SPINACH AND CARROT SOUP
CORIANDER AND PINE NUT LENTILS
MULLIGATAWNY
CHILLI CON CARNE
CHICKEN LEG QUARTERS WITH TOMATO, HONEY
AND LIME PICKLE
CHIMICHURRI STEAK
CINNAMON LAMB MEATBALLS
SAFFRON AND TOMATO RISOTTO WITH CHORIZO
SLOW-BAKED SHANKS WITH TAMARIND AND GINGER
PORK SPARE RIBS

red lentil, spinach and carrot soup

1 leek, trimmed and rinsed
40 g (1½ oz) butter
1 teaspoon finely grated fresh ginger
1 garlic clove, finely chopped
4 carrots, peeled
1.5 litres (52 fl oz/6 cups) vegetable stock
175 g (6 oz) red lentils
1 bunch English spinach, rinsed and drained
crusty bread and extra virgin olive oil, to serve

Slice the leek several times lengthways, then slice it finely.

Put the leek into a large saucepan with the butter, ginger and garlic, and sauté over medium heat until the leek is soft and lightly golden. Grate the carrot and add it to the leek along with the vegetable stock and lentils. Bring to the boil, then simmer half covered for 30 minutes. Finely slice the rinsed spinach and add it to the soup. Simmer for a further 5 minutes and season to taste with sea salt and freshly ground black pepper.

Ladle into four warm bowls and serve with crusty bread and a swirl of extra virgin olive oil.

SERVES 4

coriander and pine nut lentils

150 g (5½ oz) puy lentils
3 teaspoons sea salt
120 g (4¼ oz) cracked wheat
60 g (2¼ oz) currants
60 g (2¼ oz) butter
1 large red onion, diced
2 carrots, peeled and diced
2 teaspoons ras al hanout
150 ml (5 fl oz) chicken stock
2 handfuls of coriander (cilantro) leaves
a handful of flat-leaf (Italian) parsley leaves
60 g (2¼ oz) pine nuts, toasted

Put the lentils into a saucepan with the sea salt, cover with 500 ml (17 fl oz/2 cups) of water, and bring to the boil over high heat. Reduce the heat to medium and simmer for 35 minutes. Drain and set aside.

Put the cracked wheat and currants into a bowl and cover with boiling water. Allow them to absorb the water.

Put the butter into a large heavy-based saucepan and heat over medium heat. Add the onion and carrot and cook until the onion is soft and golden. Add the ras al hanout, the drained lentils, the cracked wheat, currants and stock. Stir well, cover, reduce the heat to low and simmer for 5 minutes.

Remove from the heat and spoon into a large serving dish. Sprinkle with the herbs and pine nuts and serve with grilled lamb cutlets.

SERVES 4

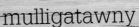

mulligatawny

2 tablespoons olive oil
500 g (1 lb 2 oz) lean shoulder of
   lamb, cut into small pieces
2 onions, finely diced
2 garlic cloves, finely chopped
1 teaspoon finely chopped fresh ginger
2 teaspoons curry powder
2 celery stalks, finely diced
70 g (2½ oz/⅓ cup) basmati rice
6 roma (plum) tomatoes, chopped
1 small red chilli, halved
1.5 litres (52 fl oz/6 cups) chicken or
   vegetable stock
200 ml (7 fl oz) coconut milk
fresh lime, yoghurt and celery leaves,
   to garnish

Heat the olive oil in a large saucepan over
medium heat, then add the diced lamb and
cook until browned. Add the onion, garlic,
ginger and curry powder, stir to combine
and cook for a further 6–7 minutes, stirring
occasionally. Stir in the celery and the rice,
then add the tomato, chilli, stock and
coconut milk. Stir, and simmer on gentle
heat for 1 hour or until the lamb is tender.

Season to taste with sea salt and freshly
ground black pepper, and serve in four
bowls with a squeeze of fresh lime,
a dollop of yoghurt and a scattering of
baby celery leaves.

SERVES 4

chilli con carne

3 teaspoons olive oil
1 large red onion, diced
3 garlic cloves, crushed
1 cinnamon stick
2 teaspoons ground cumin
2 teaspoons ground coriander
1½ teaspoons chilli flakes
750 g (1 lb 10 oz) good quality minced (ground) beef
150 g (5½ oz/1 cup) diced green capsicum (pepper)
150 g (5½ oz/1 cup) diced red capsicum (pepper)
400 g (14 oz) tin chopped tomatoes
250 g (9 oz/1 cup) tomato paste (concentrated purée)
20 g (¾ oz) dark chocolate
400 g (14 oz) tin kidney beans, drained
500 ml (17 fl oz/2 cups) beef or chicken stock

Heat the olive oil in a large saucepan over medium heat and add the onion, garlic and spices. Cook, stirring occasionally, until the onion is soft and golden brown. Add the beef mince and continue to cook until the meat is browned all over. Add the diced capsicum (pepper) and stir well to combine. Then add the tomatoes, tomato paste, chocolate, beans and stock. Cook over medium heat until the mix comes to a boil and then reduce the heat and simmer for 40 minutes. Season to taste with sea salt and freshly ground black pepper.

Spoon into four bowls and serve with warm tortillas, sour cream and guacamole.

SERVES 4

chicken leg quarters with tomato, honey and lime pickle

4 spring onions (scallions), finely sliced
4 garlic cloves, roughly chopped
400 g (14 oz) tin chopped tomatoes
2 tablespoons finely chopped Indian lime pickle
juice of 1 lemon
4 chicken leg quarters
2 tablespoons honey
a handful of coriander (cilantro) leaves
steamed rice and green salad, to serve

Preheat the oven to 180°C (350°F/Gas 4).

Put the sliced spring onions, garlic, tomatoes, pickle and lemon juice into a bowl and stir to combine.

Arrange the chicken pieces in a roasting tin and pour the sauce over. Season with sea salt, then cover the roasting tin with foil. Bake for 40 minutes, then remove the foil. Drizzle the chicken pieces with the honey and bake for a further 20 minutes.

Garnish with fresh coriander (cilantro) leaves, and serve with steamed rice and a green salad.

SERVES 4

chimichurri steak

125 ml (4 fl oz/½ cup) olive oil
1 tablespoon balsamic vinegar
30 g (1 oz/½ cup) chopped parsley
25 g (1 oz/½ cup) chopped coriander
   (cilantro) leaves
80 g (2¾ oz/½ cup) diced red
   capsicum (pepper)
4 garlic cloves, crushed
½ red onion, finely diced
1 tablespoon lime juice
½ teaspoon dried chilli flakes
4 x 185 g (6½ oz) sirloin steaks

In a bowl combine all the ingredients except the steak. Season with sea salt and freshly ground black pepper.

Heat a grill plate and cook the steaks for 4 minutes on one side over moderately high heat, turn once, and cook for a further 4 minutes. They should be nicely charred on both sides. Transfer to a warm plate, season lightly with sea salt and allow to rest for 5 minutes.

Serve the steaks with a generous spoonful of the sauce and boiled new potatoes.

SERVES 4

cinnamon lamb meatballs

500 g (1 lb 2 oz) minced (ground) lamb
2 garlic cloves, crushed
2 tablespoons finely chopped parsley
finely grated zest of 1 lemon
120 g (4¼ oz) pine nuts, roughly chopped
1 egg
60 ml (2 fl oz/¼ cup) olive oil
1 leek, white part only, trimmed, rinsed and finely sliced
400 g (14 oz) tin tomatoes
½ teaspoon ground cinnamon
1 tablespoon lemon juice

Put the lamb mince, garlic, parsley, lemon zest, pine nuts and egg into a bowl and combine well. Season with sea salt and freshly ground black pepper. Roll the mixture into small walnut-sized balls.

Heat a frying pan over high heat and add 1 tablespoon of the olive oil. Cook the meatballs in two batches until they are browned all over (3–4 minutes each batch), then remove them to a plate.

Put a small casserole or large saucepan over medium heat and add the remaining olive oil and the leek. Sauté until the leek is soft, then add the tomatoes, cinnamon and lemon juice. Add the meatballs and simmer for a further 20 minutes.

Serve with risoni or couscous and a leafy green salad.

SERVES 4

saffron and tomato risotto with chorizo

1 punnet cherry tomatoes
5 sprigs thyme
1 chorizo sausage, sliced
1 litre (35 fl oz/4 cups) chicken stock
40 g (1½ oz) butter
a pinch of saffron threads
2 garlic cloves, crushed
1 leek, white part only, rinsed and finely sliced
325 g (11½ oz/1½ cups) arborio rice
400 g (14 oz) tin chopped tomatoes
125 ml (4 fl oz/½ cup) white wine
70 g (2½ oz) parmesan cheese, freshly grated
30 g (1 oz/½ cup) roughly chopped flat-leaf (Italian) parsley leaves

Preheat the oven to 180°C (350°F/Gas 4).

Put the cherry tomatoes, thyme and sliced chorizo into a baking tin and roast in the oven for 15 minutes or until the tomatoes are beginning to split.

Meanwhile, put the chicken stock into a saucepan and bring to the boil over high heat. Reduce the heat to a low simmer.

Heat the butter in a large saucepan over medium heat. Add the saffron, garlic and leek and cook until the leek is soft and translucent. Add the rice and stir for a minute until the grains are well coated and glossy. Add the tinned tomatoes and 250 ml (9 fl oz/1 cup) of stock and simmer, stirring until it is absorbed. Repeat with another cup of stock and, when the liquid has been absorbed, add the white wine and another cup of stock. Cook until all the liquid has been absorbed and test the rice to see if it is *al dente*. If the grains are still slightly uncooked in the centre add the remaining stock and simmer until the stock has reduced and the rice is coated in a creamy sauce.

Fold the parmesan cheese through the risotto, season with freshly ground black pepper, then spoon the risotto into four warm bowls. Garnish with chorizo, cherry tomatoes and parsley.

SERVES 4

slow-baked shanks with tamarind and ginger

2 tablespoons olive oil
8 small French-trimmed lamb shanks
2 onions, peeled and roughly chopped
4 garlic cloves, finely chopped
2 teaspoons ground turmeric
1 tablespoon finely grated fresh ginger
1.25 litres (44 fl oz/5 cups) vegetable stock
90 g (3¼ oz/⅓ cup) tamarind pulp
90 g (3¼ oz/⅓ cup) tomato paste (concentrated purée)
5 ripe tomatoes, diced
a handful of coriander (cilantro) leaves, roughly chopped
1 tablespoon finely grated lemon zest

Preheat the oven to 160°C (315°F/Gas 2–3).

Heat the olive oil in a large flameproof casserole dish over medium heat. Cook the shanks in batches until golden brown. Remove from the casserole and set aside.

Add the onion, garlic, turmeric and ginger to the dish, stirring until the onion is translucent, then add the stock, tamarind pulp, tomato paste and tomatoes. Season with sea salt and freshly ground black pepper.

Return the lamb shanks to the casserole and cook, covered, in the oven for 2 hours.

Remove the casserole from the oven and divide the shanks among four warm pasta bowls. Spoon the sauce over the shanks and garnish with the coriander (cilantro) leaves and a little lemon zest.

Serve with ginger-spiced rice (see extras, page 241).

SERVES 4

pork spare ribs

2 garlic cloves, crushed
8 cm (3¼ in) piece ginger, peeled and finely grated
125 ml (4 fl oz/½ cup) kecap manis
50 g (1¾ oz/¼ cup) soft brown sugar
½ teaspoon five spice powder
1 tablespoon olive oil
16–24 American-style pork ribs
1 red capsicum (pepper), finely julienned
100 g (3½ oz) snow peas (mangetout), finely julienned
50 g (1¾ oz/¾ cup) bean sprouts
a handful of coriander (cilantro) leaves
1 tablespoon toasted sesame seeds

Put the garlic, ginger, kecap manis, brown sugar, five spice powder
and olive oil into a blender or food processor and blend to a smooth
sauce. Toss the pork ribs in the marinade and leave to marinate
overnight in the refrigerator.

Preheat the oven to 180°C (350°F/Gas 4).

Put the marinated pork ribs into a roasting tin and bake in the oven
for 30 minutes, turning them once.

Put the red capsicum (pepper), snow peas, bean sprouts and coriander
(cilantro) leaves into a bowl and toss to combine.

Divide the ribs among four serving plates and top with the salad.
Finish with a sprinkle of sesame seeds, and serve.

SERVES 4

essence

spicy hints of vanilla, ginger and honey

MELTING MOMENTS
VANILLA MACAROONS
CUPCAKES
THREE-GINGER CAKE
CARDAMOM JELLY WITH TROPICAL FRUITS
CARAMELISED FIGS WITH YOGHURT CREME
APPLE AND VANILLA SNOW
CHILLED PINEAPPLE IN VANILLA SYRUP
CHOCOLATE, CARDAMOM AND DATE PUDDINGS
ROSEMARY CREAM WITH BLOOD PLUMS

melting moments

125 g (4½ oz) unsalted butter
30 g (1 oz/¼ cup) icing
    (confectioners') sugar
110 g (3¾ oz/¾ cup) plain
    (all-purpose) flour
30 g (1 oz/¼ cup) cornflour
    (cornstarch)
1 teaspoon natural vanilla extract
icing (confectioners') sugar, extra,
    for dusting

Preheat the oven to 160°C (315°F/Gas 2–3).

Line a baking tray with baking paper.

Put the butter, icing (confectioners') sugar,
flour, cornflour and vanilla extract in a food
processor and process in short bursts until
the mixture comes together.

With lightly floured hands, roll heaped
teaspoons of the mixture into balls and
place onto the baking sheet. Flatten each
ball slightly with a floured fork.

Bake for about 15 minutes or until the
biscuits are just lightly golden brown.
Remove and cool on a wire rack.

Dust with icing (confectioners') sugar
and store in an airtight container until
ready to serve.

MAKES 20 BISCUITS
OR 10 SANDWICHED TOGETHER

vanilla macaroons

250 g (9 oz) flaked almonds
4 egg whites
300 g (10½ oz) caster (superfine)
    sugar
1 teaspoon natural vanilla extract

Preheat the oven to 180°C (350°F/Gas 4).

Line two baking trays with baking paper.

Spread the flaked almonds on a third
(unlined) baking tray and toast for
4 minutes in the oven. Remove, and set
aside to cool.

Reduce the oven temperature to
150°C (300°F/Gas 2).

Using an electric beater whisk the egg
whites and a pinch of salt until stiff. Add
the sugar gradually while still whisking,
until the mixture is thick and glossy. Add
the vanilla extract and fold in the almonds.
Drop teaspoons of the mixture onto the
prepared trays, and bake them in the oven
for 35 minutes, rotating the trays halfway
through the baking time.

Put the macaroons onto wire racks to cool,
then store in airtight containers.

MAKES 40

cupcakes

250 g (9 oz) butter, softened
125 g (4½ oz) caster (superfine) sugar
2 eggs
375 g (13 oz/2½ cups) self-raising flour, sifted
250 ml (9 fl oz/1 cup) milk
1 teaspoon natural vanilla extract

ICING
100 g (3½ oz) unsalted butter, softened
200 g (7 oz) icing (confectioners') sugar, sifted
1 teaspoon natural vanilla extract
½ teaspoon finely grated lemon zest
1 tablespoon lemon juice

Preheat the oven to 180°C (350°F/Gas 4).

Put fifteen paper cases into two patty pan or mini muffin tins.

Cream the butter and sugar until pale, then beat the eggs into the mixture one at a time. Add the flour in two batches, beating the mixture until smooth, then mix in the milk and the vanilla extract.

Spoon the batter into the paper cases and bake in the oven for 20 minutes or until the cakes are cooked through.

Remove the cupcakes to a wire rack and allow to cool.

Make the icing by stirring the butter and sifted icing (confectioners') sugar together. Add the vanilla extract and lemon zest and stir to combine. Then add the lemon juice drop by drop to form a thick spreadable consistency, or substitute with food colouring if desired. Spread the icing thickly on top of the cupcakes.

MAKES 15

three-ginger cake

200 g (7 oz/1⅓ cups) self-raising flour
1 teaspoon bicarbonate of soda (baking soda)
1 teaspoon ground ginger
125 g (4½ oz) butter
125 g (4½ oz/⅔ cup) dark brown sugar
1 teaspoon finely grated fresh ginger
125 g (4½ oz) golden syrup
2 eggs
125 ml (4 fl oz/½ cup) buttermilk
75 g (2½ oz/⅓ cup) glacé ginger, roughly chopped

Preheat the oven to 180°C (350°F/Gas 4).

Grease a 20 x 20 cm (8 x 8 in) cake tin and line it with baking paper.

Sift the flour, bicarbonate of soda and ground ginger into a bowl.

Cream the butter and brown sugar until pale, then add the fresh ginger and the golden syrup. Continue to beat for a further minute. Add the eggs one at a time, beating as you go, then beat in the dry ingredients a few spoonfuls at a time, alternating with the buttermilk. Fold in the glacé ginger and spoon the mixture into the prepared cake tin.

Bake for 35–40 minutes or until a skewer inserted into the centre comes out clean.

Serve in thick slices.

SERVES 12

cardamom jelly with tropical fruits

300 g (10½ oz) caster (superfine) sugar
4 cardamom pods, crushed
4 gelatine leaves
2 tablespoons Frangelico
12 fresh or tinned lychees, to serve
diced flesh of 1 mango, to serve
4–8 tablespoons coconut milk

Put the sugar in a small saucepan with 250 ml (9 fl oz/1 cup) of water and stir to dissolve. Put the saucepan over high heat, add the cardamom pods and bring to the boil. Cook, stirring occasionally, until the syrup turns a toffee colour and the bubbles are beginning to get smaller.

Remove from the heat and leave for a minute, then carefully stir in another 375 ml (13 fl oz/1½ cups) of water. Return to the heat and stir for a minute to ensure all the caramel has dissolved. Strain into a measuring jug, discarding the cardamom, and add enough water to ensure that you have 500 ml (17 fl oz/2 cups) of liquid. Return this liquid to the saucepan.

Soak the gelatine leaves in cold water until they soften. Squeeze the gelatine gently to remove all the water, then add the gelatine to the saucepan and cook over high heat, stirring to ensure that it dissolves into the warm caramel mixture. Remove from the heat and stir in the Frangelico.

Allow to cool, then pour into six glasses or dessert bowls. Cover, and leave to set in the refrigerator. To serve, remove from the refrigerator and allow the jelly to come to room temperature. Serve with the lychees and mango and the chilled coconut milk.

SERVES 6

caramelised figs with yoghurt creme

4 gelatine leaves
1 vanilla bean
200 ml (7 fl oz) cream
100 g (3½ oz) caster (superfine) sugar
600 g (1 lb 5 oz) plain yoghurt
6 large figs, halved
2 tablespoons caster (superfine) sugar, extra

Soak the gelatine leaves in a bowl of cold water for a few minutes. Rub the vanilla bean between your fingertips until it is soft, then slice it in half lengthways.

Put the cream into a small saucepan with the caster (superfine) sugar and the vanilla bean. Heat over low heat, stirring until the sugar has dissolved. Remove from the heat. Squeeze any excess moisture from the softened gelatine and add it to the warm cream. Stir until the gelatine has completely dissolved. Scrape the inside of the vanilla bean to remove all the seeds and stir them into the cream.

Put the yoghurt into a large bowl and gently whisk. Add the warm cream mixture to the yoghurt and continue to whisk until the pudding mixture is smooth.

Rinse six dariole moulds or ramekins in cold water and shake to remove any excess water. Divide the creamy yoghurt mixture among the moulds, ensuring that the tops are level, and refrigerate until set.

Sprinkle the fig halves with the extra caster (superfine) sugar and place them under a hot grill for a few minutes or until the sugar is golden brown.

To serve, dip the base of each mould into warm water, then turn the puddings out onto six dessert plates and serve with the grilled figs.

SERVES 6

apple and vanilla snow

1 vanilla bean
6 green cooking apples, peeled and finely sliced
75 g ($\frac{1}{3}$ cup) caster (superfine) sugar, plus 2 tablespoons extra
1 tablespoon lemon juice
2 egg whites
almond bread, to serve

Rub the vanilla bean between your fingertips to soften, then slice it in half lengthways.

Put the apple, vanilla bean, 75 g ($\frac{1}{3}$ cup) of caster (superfine) sugar, the lemon juice and 125 ml (4 fl oz/$\frac{1}{2}$ cup) of water into a saucepan over medium heat. Cook for 20 minutes or until the apples have dissolved into a soft purée. Remove and allow to cool.

Beat the egg whites until they form stiff peaks, then add the 2 tablespoons of caster (superfine) sugar and beat until glossy and firm. Fold the cooled apple through the egg whites and spoon into bowls. Chill until ready to serve.

Serve with almond bread.

SERVES 4

chilled pineapple in vanilla syrup

1 vanilla bean
220 g (7¾ oz/1 cup) sugar
1 large, ripe pineapple
juice and grated zest of 1 lime
vanilla ice cream, to serve

Rub the vanilla bean between your fingertips to soften, then slice it in half lengthways. Put the vanilla bean into a small saucepan with the sugar and 500 ml (17 fl oz/2 cups) of water and bring to the boil over high heat. Reduce the heat and simmer until the sugar has dissolved, then remove from the heat and allow to cool.

Slice away the skin of the pineapple and cut the flesh into bite-sized chunks. Put the pineapple pieces into a bowl and add the vanilla syrup, lime zest and lime juice. Toss to combine, then chill.

When ready to serve, spoon the cold pineapple into four chilled bowls and drizzle with the vanilla syrup. Serve with a scoop of vanilla ice cream.

SERVES 6

chocolate, cardamom and date puddings

185 g (6½ oz) pitted dates
125 g (4½ oz) butter, cubed
100 g (3½ oz) good quality dark eating chocolate
2 eggs
185 g (6½ oz/1 cup) dark brown sugar
150 g (5½ oz/1 cup) self-raising flour
1 teaspoon ground cardamom
2 tablespoons crushed pistachios, to serve
thick (double/heavy) cream, to serve
4 extra squares of chocolate (optional)

Preheat the oven to 180°C (350°F/Gas 4).

Butter four small (250 ml/9 fl oz/1 cup) soufflé dishes.

Put the dates in a saucepan with 250 ml (9 fl oz/1 cup) of water and soften over a gentle heat. Mash the dates with a fork, then add the butter and the chocolate. Continue to cook until the chocolate and butter have melted, then remove from the heat.

Beat the eggs with the brown sugar in a bowl, then add the chocolate mix. Whisk to combine, then stir the flour and ground cardamom through.

Pour the mixture into the four buttered soufflé dishes and place the dishes in a baking tin. Pour water into the baking tin, making sure it comes halfway up the sides of the soufflé dishes. Cover the baking tin with a sheet of buttered foil. Bake for 35–40 minutes.

Remove the baking tin from the oven and carefully lift out the soufflé dishes. Serve the puddings warm with crushed pistachios and cream. For an extra chocolate hit, press a square of chocolate into the centre of each hot pudding before serving.

SERVES 4

rosemary cream with blood plums

200 ml (7 fl oz) milk
1 vanilla bean
1 sprig rosemary
125 g (4½ oz) caster (superfine) sugar
3 egg yolks
8 blood plums, halved and stones removed
2 tablespoons brown sugar
juice of 1 orange
300 g (10½ oz) thick (double/heavy) cream

Put the milk into a small saucepan over low heat. Rub the vanilla bean between your fingertips, then cut it in half lengthways. Add the split bean to the milk with the sprig of rosemary. Allow the milk to simmer for 10 minutes, then remove and strain into a jug.

Whisk the egg yolks with the caster (superfine) sugar in a separate bowl, then whisk in the warm milk. Pour into a clean saucepan and stir over medium heat for 8–10 minutes or until the mixture coats the back of the spoon. Pour into a clean bowl and allow to cool. Cover and refrigerate until ready to serve.

Put the plums into a saucepan with the brown sugar and orange juice. Cook over medium heat until the plums are beginning to soften. Remove from the heat and allow the plums to sit in the warm syrup.

Divide the plums among four bowls. Fold the cream through the chilled custard and spoon over the plums.

SERVES 4

sweet

chocolate and fruit, sugar and spice

LITTLE CHOCOLATE MOUSSE CUPS
BLUEBERRY SLICE WITH VANILLA CREME FRAICHE
CHOCOLATE BROWNIES
RASPBERRY GRANITA
BAKED PEACHES WITH COCONUT AND BROWN SUGAR
PINEAPPLE AND COCONUT ICE WITH CHILLI GLASS
WHITE VELVET CAKE WITH PASSIONFRUIT
BAKED CHAI CUSTARDS
CINNAMON CRUMBED APPLES
FIG AND FILO PARCELS WITH A POMEGRANATE SYRUP

little chocolate mousse cups

165 g (5¾ oz) good quality dark
  chocolate
25 g (1 oz) unsalted butter
185 ml (6 fl oz/¾ cup) cream
1 teaspoon ground cinnamon
1 teaspoon natural vanilla extract
2 tablespoons caster (superfine) sugar
3 egg yolks
2 tablespoons cocoa

Melt the chocolate and butter in the top
of a double boiler over medium heat, stir
to combine, then remove from the heat
and allow to cool.

Whip the cream to soft peaks, gently fold
the cinnamon and vanilla extract through,
and set aside in the refrigerator.

Combine the sugar, 60 ml (2 fl oz/¼ cup)
of water and the egg yolks in the top of
a double boiler over medium heat and
whisk until thick and foamy, ensuring
the yolks are cooked—about 5 minutes.
Allow to cool.

Fold the egg yolk mixture into the
chocolate, combine evenly, then fold in
the chilled whipped cream.

Pour into eight demitasse cups and chill
for 4 hours before serving. Serve dusted
with cocoa.

SERVES 8

blueberry slice with vanilla crème fraiche

100 g (3½ oz/1 cup) pecan nuts
250 g (9 oz) caster (superfine) sugar
100 g (3½ oz/⅔ cup) self-raising flour
grated zest of 1 lemon
150 g (5½ oz) butter, melted
4 egg whites
100 g (3½ oz/⅔ cup) blueberries
250 g (9 oz/1 cup) crème fraiche
½ teaspoon natural vanilla extract

Preheat the oven to 150°C (300°F/Gas 2).

Grease a 15 x 30 cm (6 x 12 in) or 22 cm (8½ in) square baking tin and line it with baking paper.

Put the pecan nuts into a food processor and pulse several times to break them into small pieces. Add the sugar, flour and lemon zest and process for a minute. Remove the dry ingredients to a bowl and stir the melted butter through.

Whisk the egg whites until soft peaks form, then fold them through the thick pecan batter. Pour the mixture into the prepared tin and scatter the blueberries over the top.

Bake for 25–30 minutes, rotating the tin after 15 minutes. Allow to cool in the tin.

Put the crème fraiche into a bowl and very gently fold the vanilla extract through.

Cut the slice into rectangles or squares and serve with a dollop of vanilla crème fraiche.

MAKES 9

chocolate brownies

140 g (5 oz/1 cup) hazelnuts
335 g (11¾ oz/1½ cups) sugar
4 eggs
60 g (2¼ oz/½ cup) unsweetened cocoa powder
80 g (2¾ oz/½ cup) self-raising flour
1 tablespoon natural vanilla extract
½ teaspoon salt
250 g (9 oz) butter, melted
100 g (3½ oz) dark chocolate, roughly chopped
100 g (3½ oz) white chocolate, roughly chopped

Preheat the oven to 175°C (335°F/Gas 3–4).

Grease a 23 x 30 cm (9 x 12 in) baking tin and line it with baking paper.

Put the hazelnuts onto a separate baking tray and roast in the oven until golden brown. Remove from the oven and put the hazelnuts onto a clean tea towel (dish towel). Gather up the towel and rub the hazelnuts together to remove the outer husks. Discard the husks and roughly chop the hazelnuts.

Put the sugar and eggs into a large bowl and whisk until the mixture is pale and creamy. Add the cocoa powder, flour, vanilla extract and salt, and whisk to combine. Slowly add the melted butter and stir until all the ingredients are well combined. Stir the chopped chocolate and the chopped hazelnuts through the mix and pour into the prepared baking tin. Bake for 25–30 minutes.

Remove and allow to cool. Cut into small squares and store in an airtight container.

MAKES 20

raspberry granita

500 g (1 lb 2 oz/4 cups) frozen raspberries
335 g (11¾ oz/1½ cups) caster (superfine) sugar
juice of ½ a lime
100 ml (3½ fl oz) vodka

Heat the raspberries in a saucepan with the sugar and 750 ml (26 fl oz/3 cups) of water. Cook over low heat for 8 minutes, then remove from the heat. Crush the berries into the liquid and strain through a fine sieve. Discard the berry pulp.

Add the lime juice and vodka to the berry syrup and pour it into a wide, shallow container. Freeze for an hour.

Using a fork, scrape the ice from the sides of the container back into the mixture. Return to the freezer for another hour. Repeat this process three times, until the granita looks like crushed ice.

Serve the granita spooned into four chilled glasses.

SERVES 4

baked peaches with coconut and brown sugar

4 ripe peaches
60 g (2¼ oz/⅓ cup) palm sugar
    (jaggery) or dark brown sugar
20 g (¾ oz/⅓ cup) shredded coconut
1 teaspoon natural vanilla extract
vanilla ice cream, to serve

Preheat the oven to 180°C (350°F/Gas 4).

Halve the peaches and remove the stones. Put the peaches onto a baking tray flesh side up.

In a small bowl combine the palm sugar, coconut and vanilla extract and with your fingertips rub together to combine. Spoon the coconut mixture into the centre of each of the peaches. Bake in the oven for 20 minutes.

Put the warm peaches into four dessert bowls and serve with a scoop of vanilla ice cream.

SERVES 4

pineapple and coconut ice with chilli glass

250 g (9 oz) diced fresh pineapple
55 g (2 oz/¼ cup) caster (superfine) sugar
400 ml (14 fl oz) coconut cream

CHILLI GLASS
150 g (5½ oz/⅔ cup) caster (superfine) sugar
½ teaspoon chilli flakes

Line an 8 x 16 cm (3¼ x 6¼ in) loaf (bar) tin with baking paper or plastic wrap.

Put the diced pineapple and sugar into a small saucepan and cook over medium heat for 10 minutes. Remove from the heat and allow to cool.

Stir the pineapple into the coconut cream, then pour the mix into the lined loaf tin. Freeze for 4 hours or overnight.

To make the chilli glass, line a baking tray with baking paper. Put the sugar and chilli flakes into a small saucepan and heat over low heat until the sugar melts. You may need to swirl the sugar over the base of the saucepan to help it melt, but don't stir it with a spoon. When the sugar has melted completely and has turned into a golden brown toffee, remove it from the heat and pour it onto the lined baking tray. Tip the tray a little to ensure the toffee coats the tray evenly and thinly.

To serve, turn the ice cream out onto a clean surface and cut into six slices. Transfer to six chilled plates and top with shards of the cracked chilli glass.

SERVES 6

white velvet cake with passionfruit

135 g (4¾ oz) white chocolate
125 g (4½ oz) unsalted butter
4 eggs, separated
90 g (3¼ oz) sugar
60 g (2¼ oz) plain (all-purpose) flour
200 ml (7 fl oz) cream, whipped
pulp of 4 passionfruit

Preheat the oven to 180°C (350°F/Gas 4).

Grease a 20 cm (8 in) round cake tin and line it with baking paper.

Put the chocolate and butter into a bowl over a small saucepan of water and melt over very low heat. Remove from the heat.

With electric beaters, whisk the egg whites until soft peaks form, then add the sugar and continue to whisk until the whites are firm and glossy.

Put the warm chocolate mixture into a bowl and add the egg yolks one at a time while continuously whisking. Add the flour to the chocolate mixture and gently stir to combine. Gently fold together the chocolate mixture and the egg whites. Spoon into the prepared cake tin and bake for 20 minutes or until firm.

Allow the cake to cool in the tin, then turn it out onto a serving plate. Spoon whipped cream over the top of the cake and drizzle with fresh passionfruit.

SERVES 8

baked chai custards

6 cardamom pods
4 whole cloves
½ teaspoon white peppercorns
1 cinnamon stick
250 ml (9 fl oz/1 cup) milk
300 ml (10½ fl oz) cream
45 g (1½ oz/½ cup) desiccated coconut
2 cm (¾ in) piece ginger, peeled and sliced
1 English Breakfast teabag
3 eggs
2 egg yolks
90 g (3¼ oz/¼ cup) honey
fresh fruit and cocoa powder, to serve

Preheat the oven to 180°C (350°F/Gas 4).

Roughly crush the spices using a mortar and pestle, just to release their flavours and aromas. Put the spices in a heavy-based saucepan with the milk, cream, coconut, ginger and teabag. Heat over medium heat, stirring gently, reducing the heat just before the mixture comes to the boil. Remove from the heat and allow to steep for 10 minutes. Strain into a jug.

In a bowl, whisk together the eggs, egg yolks and honey. Pour the strained cream and milk over the eggs, and whisk to combine. Pour the custard through a strainer into the jug.

Place a folded tea towel (dish towel) into the base of a deep baking dish. Sit six small tea cups on the tea towel and fill them with the custard. Fill the baking dish with water until the water comes halfway up the sides of the cups. Bake in the oven for 40–50 minutes or until the custard has set. Remove, and chill in the refrigerator until ready to serve.

Serve with a dusting of cocoa, and fresh fruit.

SERVES 6

cinnamon crumbed apples

150 g (5½ oz/2½ cups) fresh breadcrumbs
95 g (3¼ oz/½ cup) soft brown sugar
2 teaspoons ground cinnamon
juice and grated zest of 1 orange
50 g (1¾ oz) butter
6 green cooking apples, peeled, cored and sliced into thin
   wedges
55 g (2 oz/¼ cup) caster (superfine) sugar
whipped cream, to serve

Preheat the oven to 180°C (350°F/Gas 4).

Line a baking tray with baking paper.

In a small bowl combine the breadcrumbs, brown sugar, cinnamon
and orange zest.

Heat the butter in a shallow heavy-based saucepan over low heat and
pour it over the crumbs. Spread the buttery crumbs over the lined
baking tray. Bake in the oven for 8–10 minutes or until the crumbs are
crisp. Remove and allow to cool.

Place the sliced apple in a heavy-based saucepan and add the orange
juice and caster (superfine) sugar. Cover with a lid and cook over low
heat for 10 minutes, stirring occasionally, until the apples are soft. If
necessary, add 60 ml (2 fl oz/¼ cup) of water.

Spoon the cooked apple into six bowls, top with the fragrant crumbs
and serve with whipped cream.

SERVES 6

fig and filo parcels with a pomegranate syrup

80 g (2¾ oz/¾ cup) ground almonds
6 dried figs, finely chopped
2 tablespoons honey
2 teaspoons finely grated lemon zest
2 teaspoons lemon juice
1 teaspoon ground cinnamon
¼ teaspoon ground cardamom
3 sheets filo pastry
40 g (1½ oz) butter, melted
2 tablespoons icing (confectioners') sugar
250 ml (9 fl oz/1 cup) fresh pomegranate juice
110 g (3¾ oz/½ cup) caster (superfine) sugar
thick (double/heavy) cream and fresh pomegranate, to serve

Preheat the oven to 180°C (350°F/Gas 4).

Line a baking tray with baking paper.

In a bowl combine the ground almonds, figs, honey, lemon zest, lemon juice, cinnamon and cardamom.

Put one of the sheets of filo on a clean dry surface and brush with some of the melted butter. Cover with another sheet of filo and butter the surface again before repeating with the final sheet of filo. Cut the sheet of filo in half lengthways, then into thirds (you should have six small rectangles). Spread the ground almond mixture over the rectangles, leaving 1 cm (½ in) clear at the end of each rectangle. Roll them up to form six tight rolls. Brush any remaining butter over the rolls before placing them on the prepared baking tray. Bake for about 5 minutes each side or until they are golden brown all over. Remove to a cooling rack and dust with icing (confectioners') sugar.

Put the pomegranate juice and caster (superfine) sugar into a small saucepan and bring to the boil. Continue to cook until the juice has reduced by half and has formed a syrup.

Serve the filo fingers with a dollop of cream, a drizzle of pomegranate syrup and a scatter of fresh pomegranate seeds.

SERVES 6

citrus

sugary lemon, lime and orange

LEMON DELICIOUS CUPS
ORANGE SALAD
MANDARIN BUTTERFLY CAKES
PAPAYA WITH LEMONGRASS SYRUP
LIME PARFAIT
LEMON BUTTER COOKIES
BAKED RICOTTA CHEESECAKE WITH PASSIONFRUIT
BLOOD ORANGE JELLY WITH GINGER CRUMBS
LIME AND COCONUT TART
RUBY GRAPEFRUIT SORBET WITH MORELLO CHERRIES

lemon delicious cups

60 g (2¼ oz) butter
juice and grated zest of 2 lemons
275 g (9¾ oz/1¼ cups) caster (superfine) sugar
3 eggs, separated
1 teaspoon natural vanilla extract
35 g (1¼ oz/¼ cup) self-raising flour
375 ml (13 fl oz/1½ cups) milk
whipped cream, to serve

Preheat the oven to 180°C (350°F/Gas 4).

Lightly butter six tea cups.

Cream the butter with the lemon zest and sugar, then add the egg yolks and vanilla extract. Stir in the flour and milk alternately to make a smooth batter. Add the lemon juice and ensure that it is stirred well into the batter.

In a separate bowl whisk the egg whites until they form stiff peaks, then fold the whites through the batter. Pour this mixture into the six tea cups.

Sit the cups in a baking tin and fill the tin with water to halfway up the sides of the cups. Bake for 25 minutes.

Serve with a dollop of whipped cream.

SERVES 6

orange salad

navel oranges
teaspoons finely grated fresh ginger
teaspoons soft brown sugar
teaspoons honey
tablespoons Grand Marnier
mon sorbet, to serve

ith a sharp knife remove the top and bottom of the oranges, then
t away the skin on the sides, making sure that you remove all the
hite pith. Thinly slice the oranges crossways, removing any seeds,
d put the orange slices into a deep dish. Scatter the ginger and
own sugar over them, then drizzle with the honey. Pour the Grand
arnier over, cover and refrigerate until ready to serve.

rve with lemon sorbet.

RVES 4

mandarin butterfly cakes

3 mandarins
6 eggs
150 g (5½ oz/⅔ cup) caster (superfine) sugar
185 g (6½ oz/1¾ cups) ground almonds
1 teaspoon baking powder
250 g (9 oz) mascarpone cheese
2 tablespoons icing (confectioners') sugar,
    plus extra for dusting
½ teaspoon orange flower water

Preheat the oven to 180°C (350°F/Gas 4).

Line cupcake trays with fifteen paper cases.

Wash the unpeeled mandarins and put them into a large saucepan.
Cover them with water, bring to the boil and cook for 2 hours. Drain
the mandarins, allow them to cool, then break them into segments
and remove the seeds.

Put the fruit, including the peel, into a food processor and purée.
Beat the eggs until light and fluffy, then add the caster (superfine)
sugar and beat for a further minute before folding in the ground
almonds, baking powder and mandarin purée. Spoon the mixture into
the prepared cupcake papers and bake for 20 minutes. Remove, and
allow to cool in the tin.

Put the mascarpone, icing (confectioners') sugar and orange flower
water into a bowl and stir to combine.

When the cakes have cooled, slice into the top of each cupcake to
create a well. Spoon the mascarpone into the centre. Cut the removed
piece of cake in half and arrange the pieces on top of the mascarpone
so that they look like butterfly wings. Dust the cupcakes with the
extra icing (confectioners') sugar.

MAKES 15 CUPCAKES

papaya with lemongrass syrup

220 g (7¾ oz/1 cup) sugar
80 ml (2½ fl oz/⅓ cup) lemongrass
  tea
125 g (4½ oz/½ cup) passionfruit pulp
2 small red papayas
lime wedges, to serve

Put the sugar and lemongrass tea into a saucepan with 375 ml (13 fl oz/1½ cups) of water. Bring to the boil, then reduce the heat and simmer for 15 minutes. Remove from the heat, strain into a bowl and add the passionfruit pulp. Allow to cool, then cover and refrigerate until ready to use.

Slice the papaya into four chilled bowls and spoon the lemongrass syrup over.

Serve with a wedge of lime and a scoop of vanilla ice cream.

SERVES 4

lime parfait

juice and finely grated zest of 3 limes
90 g (3¼ oz) caster (superfine) sugar
5 egg yolks
300 g (10½ oz) crème fraiche
fresh summer fruits, to serve

Line an 8 x 16 cm (3¼ x 6¼ in) loaf (bar) tin with baking paper or plastic wrap.

Put the lime juice and sugar into a small saucepan and bring to the boil. Boil for 3 minutes until the mixture becomes a thick, clear syrup.

Meanwhile, whisk the egg yolks with electric beaters to double their volume, then slowly pour the hot lime syrup over the yolks, whisking continuously. Continue to whisk until the mixture has cooled. Lightly fold the crème fraiche and lime zest into the egg yolks. Pour the mixture into the prepared tin and freeze for at least 2 hours before serving.

Serve sliced with a tumble of fresh summer fruits.

SERVES 6

lemon butter cookies

125 g (4½ oz) unsalted butter, chilled
    and cut into small cubes
120 g (4¼ oz) caster (superfine) sugar
finely grated zest of 2 lemons
3 egg whites
juice of 1 lemon
165 g (5¾ oz) semolina
60 g (2¼ oz) ground almonds
1 teaspoon baking powder
icing (confectioners') sugar, for dusting

Preheat the oven to 180°C (350°F/Gas 4).

Grease and flour a 20 x 30 cm (8 x 12 in)
baking tray.

Cream the butter and caster (superfine)
sugar with the lemon zest, then add
the egg whites, lemon juice, semolina,
ground almonds and baking powder.
Combine well.

Press the mixture evenly into the prepared
baking tray and bake for 20–25 minutes.

Remove from the oven and, while the
mixture is still warm, cut it into hearts
using a small heart-shaped cookie cutter.
Dust with icing (confectioners') sugar.

MAKES 15

baked ricotta cheesecake with passionfruit

4 eggs, separated
110 g (3¾ oz/½ cup) caster (superfine) sugar
500 g (1 lb 2 oz/2 cups) firm ricotta cheese
juice and grated zest of 2 lemons
1 teaspoon natural vanilla extract
125 g (4½ oz/½ cup) passionfruit pulp
125 ml (4 fl oz/½ cup) cream
75 g (2½ oz/½ cup) plain (all-purpose) flour
icing (confectioners') sugar, for dusting
cream and fresh passionfruit, to serve

Preheat the oven to 180°C (350°F/Gas 4).

Grease and line a 20 cm (8 in) springform tin.

Beat the egg yolks and caster (superfine) sugar until they are pale and creamy, then fold in the ricotta cheese, lemon juice, lemon zest, vanilla extract, passionfruit pulp and cream. Fold to combine well. Sift the flour over the mixture, then fold it into the batter.

Whisk the egg whites until soft peaks form, then lightly fold the egg whites into the mixture. Pour the batter into the prepared cake tin and bake in the oven for 40 minutes. Put a layer of foil over the cake to stop it burning, and bake for a further 15 minutes.

Cool in the tin before transferring to a serving plate.

Dust with icing (confectioners') sugar and serve with a drizzle of cream and fresh passionfruit.

SERVES 8–10

blood orange jelly with ginger crumbs

500 ml (17 fl oz/2 cups) blood orange juice, strained
75 g (2½ oz/⅓ cup) caster (superfine) sugar
4 gelatine leaves

GINGER CRUMBS
40 g (1½ oz/½ cup) fresh breadcrumbs
55 g (2 oz/½ cup) ground almonds
1½ teaspoons ground ginger
50 g (1¾ oz/¼ cup) soft brown sugar
20 g (¾ oz) butter, melted
cream, to serve

Put the orange juice into a small saucepan with the caster (superfine) sugar. Cook over medium heat, stirring until the sugar has dissolved. Remove from the heat.

Soak the gelatine leaves in cold water until they are soft. Squeeze to remove any excess water, then put the gelatine into the warm orange juice. Stir until the gelatine has dissolved, then pour the juice into a bowl. Cover with plastic wrap and chill for 3–4 hours or overnight.

To make the ginger crumbs preheat the oven to 180°C (350°F/Gas 4). Line a baking tray with baking paper.

Put all the ingredients into a bowl and rub together until the mixture resembles moist breadcrumbs. Put the crumbs onto the baking tray and bake in the oven, stirring occasionally, for 10 minutes or until the crumbs are golden brown and crisp. Remove and cool before storing in an airtight container.

Spoon the jelly into four serving bowls or parfait glasses. Drizzle with cream and top with the ginger crumbs.

SERVES 4

lime and coconut tart

125 g (4½ oz/½ cup) unsalted butter, softened
335 g (11¾ oz/1½ cups) caster (superfine) sugar
4 large eggs
165 g (5¾ oz) plain yoghurt
1 teaspoon natural vanilla extract
60 ml (2 fl oz/¼ cup) lime juice
2 tablespoons finely grated lime zest
60 g (2¼ oz/1 cup) shredded coconut
1 pre-baked 23 cm (9 in) shortcrust pastry tart case (see
    extras, page 244)
icing (confectioners') sugar, for dusting
cream, to serve

Preheat the oven to 170°C (325°F/Gas 3).

Put the butter and caster (superfine) sugar into a food processor and
process until they have come together. Add the eggs one at a time
until they are well incorporated, then add the yoghurt, vanilla extract,
lime juice and lime zest. Don't worry if the mixture looks as though it
has split. Pour it into a large jug or bowl and stir the coconut through,
then pour into the prepared tart case.

Bake for 35–40 minutes or until the filling is golden and puffed.

Dust with icing (confectioners') sugar and serve with cream.

SERVES 8–10

ruby grapefruit sorbet with morello cherries

220 g (7¾ oz/1 cup) sugar
2 star anise
750 ml (26 fl oz/3 cups) freshly
    squeezed ruby grapefruit juice
bottled morello cherries, to serve

Put the sugar, star anise and 250 ml
(9 fl oz/1 cup) of water in a saucepan over
medium heat and bring to the boil. Stir
until the sugar has dissolved, then remove
from the heat.

Meanwhile, put the grapefruit juice in a
large bowl. Pour the sugar syrup over the
juice, remove the star anise and allow to
cool at room temperature. Pour into a
plastic container, cover with plastic wrap
and freeze for 3 hours or overnight.

Remove the sorbet from the freezer and
scoop into a food processor or blender.
Blend to a smooth consistency, then return
to the freezer until ready to serve.

Scoop the sorbet into four bowls and top
with the morello cherries.

SERVES 4

blossom

floral aromas and springtime desserts

ROSE-SCENTED ETON MESS
LEMON AND ROSEWATER SHERBET
MANGO LASSI
ORANGE FLOWER MADELEINES
MERINGUE ROULADE
STRAWBERRY ROSEWATER MARSHMALLOWS
POACHED APRICOTS WITH HONEY LAVENDER CUSTARD
HONEY AND ORANGE FLOWER SYRUP FRUIT SALAD
RASPBERRY AND ROSEWATER JELLY
SPICED BISCUITS WITH ICED TEA

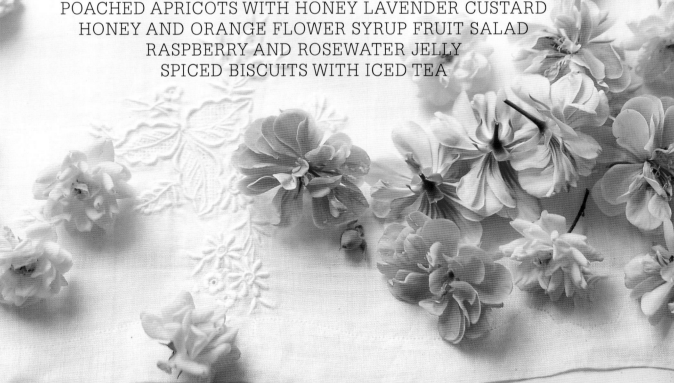

rose-scented eton mess

2 egg whites
100 g (3½ oz) caster (superfine) sugar
2 punnets strawberries
2 teaspoons rosewater
2 tablespoons icing (confectioners') sugar
300 ml (10½ fl oz) cream, whipped

Preheat the oven to 120°C (235°F/Gas ½).

Line a baking tray with baking paper.

Using electric beaters whisk the egg whites until soft peaks form. Add half the caster (superfine) sugar and continue to whisk until the mixture is glossy, then add the remaining caster sugar. Continue to whisk until all the sugar has been incorporated into the mix.

Spoon dollops of the meringue mixture onto the baking tray to form six meringues and bake in the oven for 1½ hours. Remove the meringues to a wire rack and allow to cool. Store in an airtight container until ready to use.

Hull and dice the strawberries and put them into a bowl with the rosewater and sifted icing (confectioners') sugar. Stir to combine, and allow to marinate for 10 minutes.

Smash the meringues and layer them in a trifle bowl with the whipped cream and the strawberries, and serve immediately.

SERVES 6

lemon and rosewater sherbet

35 g (1¼ oz/⅓ cup) ground almonds
220 g (7¾ oz/1 cup) sugar
4 cardamom pods, split
1 teaspoon rosewater
80 ml (2½ fl oz/⅓ cup) lemon juice
1 teaspoon grenadine (optional)

Put the ground almonds, sugar and cardamom pods into a saucepan with 250 ml (9 fl oz/1 cup) of water. Boil over high heat until the mixture thickens. Allow to cool, then add the rosewater, lemon juice and grenadine, if using. Stir to combine.

Use as a syrup poured over ice and topped with sparkling water.

SERVES 10

mango lassi

235 g (8½ oz/¾ cup) roughly chopped mango
1 teaspoon honey
1 teaspoon lime juice
125 g (4½ oz/½ cup) plain yoghurt
205 g (7¼ oz/1½ cups) ice cubes

Put all the ingredients into a blender and blend until smooth.

Pour into two chilled glasses and serve.

MAKES 2

orange flower madeleines

2 eggs, separated
60 g (2¼ oz) unsalted butter, softened
110 g (3¾ oz/½ cup) sugar
⅛ teaspoon salt
⅛ teaspoon baking powder
½ teaspoon grated orange zest
juice of ½ an orange
½ teaspoon orange flower water
½ teaspoon natural vanilla extract
110 g (3¾ oz/¾ cup) plain (all-purpose) flour
⅛ teaspoon cream of tartar

Preheat the oven to 150°C (300°F/Gas 2).

Brush a madeleine tin with melted butter.

Beat the egg whites until firm. Set aside.

Cream the butter and sugar until light and fluffy, then add the egg yolks one at a time, beating to combine. Add the salt, baking powder, grated orange zest, orange juice, orange flower water and the vanilla extract. Fold lightly to combine. Slowly add the flour and mix until the batter is smooth. Stir in the cream of tartar. Fold 1 cup of the batter through the egg whites, then fold the remaining batter through.

Drop tablespoons of the mixture into the prepared madeleine moulds. Bake for 10 minutes or until firm and golden. Tip the madeleines onto a wire rack to cool, and repeat with the remaining batter. Dust lightly with icing (confectioners') sugar and store in an airtight container.

MAKES 50

meringue roulade

5 egg whites
150 g (5½ oz) caster (superfine) sugar, plus
    extra for sprinkling
2 teaspoons cornflour (cornstarch)
1 teaspoon natural vanilla extract
1 teaspoon white vinegar
2 punnets raspberries
1 teaspoon orange flower water
200 ml (7 fl oz) cream, whipped
icing (confectioners') sugar, to serve

Preheat the oven to 160°C (315°F/Gas 2–3).

Line a baking tray with baking paper.

Beat the egg whites until soft peaks form, then slowly add the 150 g
(5½ oz) caster (superfine) sugar and whisk until it has dissolved and
the mixture is smooth and glossy. Fold in the cornflour, vanilla extract
and vinegar, then spread the meringue evenly over the baking tray.

Bake for 20 minutes, then remove from the oven and flip over onto a
sheet of baking paper sprinkled with a little caster (superfine) sugar.
With the short side facing you, roll the meringue and baking sheet up,
like a Swiss roll. Allow to sit until cool, then unroll.

Put the raspberries into a bowl and sprinkle with the orange flower
water. Toss several times to ensure the essence is blended through
most of the berries. Spread the whipped cream over the meringue,
leaving 3 cm (1¼ in) clear at one end, and cover with the berries.
Roll the meringue up again and sprinkle it with icing (confectioners')
sugar. Cut into six thick slices, and serve.

SERVES 6

strawberry rosewater marshmallows

1 punnet strawberries, rinsed, hulled and quartered
2 teaspoons rosewater
500 g (1 lb 2 oz) caster (superfine) sugar
2 egg whites
20 g (¾ oz) powdered gelatine
icing (confectioners') sugar, for dusting
fresh strawberries and dark chocolate, to serve

Grease a 20 x 30 cm (8 x 12 in) baking tray and dust it with icing (confectioners') sugar.

Gently heat the strawberries in a saucepan with the rosewater until the fruit becomes mushy. Mash with a fork, then strain, pushing the pulp through a sieve to form a thick purée. Set aside.

Put the caster (superfine) sugar into a saucepan with 250 ml (9 fl oz/1 cup) of water and stir over low heat to dissolve. Increase the heat to medium and boil the syrup until it reaches 125°C (257°F). This will take approximately 20 minutes.

While the syrup is heating, beat the egg whites until soft peaks form. Set aside.

Once the syrup reaches the required temperature pour a little over the strawberry purée, quickly add the gelatine and mix thoroughly, ensuring no lumps remain. Then add the remaining syrup and stir through. Pour the strawberry syrup onto the beaten egg whites and beat with an electric beater at medium speed until the mixture doubles in volume. Beat continuously for 5–8 minutes until thick and fluffy. The mix should be 40°C (104°F) maximum at this point.

Pour the mixture into the prepared tray and allow it to stand at room temperature for at least 3 hours until the marshmallow is set.

Cut into small squares, roll in extra icing (confectioners') sugar and serve with fresh strawberries and shards of bitter chocolate.

MAKES 48 SQUARES

poached apricots with honey lavender custard

500 ml (17 fl oz/2 cups) milk
2 tablespoons honey
2 teaspoons lavender petals
4 egg yolks
75 g (2½ oz/⅓ cup) caster (superfine) sugar

poached apricots
110 g (3¾ oz/½ cup) caster (superfine) sugar
1 vanilla bean, halved
8 apricots, halved and stones removed

Put the milk, honey and lavender into a small saucepan and heat over low heat until warm. Whisk together the egg yolks and sugar until light and creamy. Slowly add the warm milk to the bowl, whisking as you pour. Rinse out the saucepan and dry thoroughly before pouring the mixture back into the saucepan through a fine sieve. Stir over medium heat until the custard coats the back of a wooden spoon. Remove from the heat and pour into a clean, chilled bowl or jug.

To poach the apricots, put the sugar and the vanilla bean into a saucepan with 375 ml (13 fl oz/1½ cups) of water. Bring to the boil over high heat, reduce the heat and simmer for a few minutes before adding the apricots. Cook the apricots for 5 minutes or until they are soft, then remove from the heat.

Divide the apricots among four dessert bowls and pour the honey lavender custard over.

SERVES 4

honey and orange flower syrup fruit salad

75 g (2½ oz/⅓ cup) sugar
2 tablespoons lime juice
¼ teaspoon orange flower water
1 tablespoon honey
1 large mango, flesh diced
1 red papaya, peeled, seeded and cut into wedges
4 passionfruit, halved
2 peaches, stones removed, and sliced

Put the sugar in a small saucepan with 250 ml (9 fl oz/1 cup) of water and bring to the boil over high heat. Reduce the heat and simmer for 5 minutes, stirring occasionally to ensure that the sugar completely dissolves. Take the pan off the heat and allow to cool completely. Stir in the lime juice, orange flower water and honey, then pour the syrup into a glass bowl or jug and refrigerate until ready to use.

Divide the fruit among four bowls and drizzle with some of the syrup.

SERVES 4

raspberry and rosewater jelly

250 g (9 oz/2 cups) raspberries, fresh or frozen
juice of 1 orange
85 g (3 oz) caster (superfine) sugar
½ teaspoon rosewater
4 gelatine leaves
cream and fresh berries, to serve

Put the raspberries, orange juice, sugar and 500 ml (17 fl oz/2 cups) of water in a saucepan and heat over medium heat until it is simmering gently, then cook the fruit for another 5 minutes. Remove from the heat, strain into a measuring jug and add the rosewater. Soak the gelatine leaves in a bowl of cold water. When soft squeeze any excess water from the gelatine and stir it through the warm liquid.

Pour into four serving bowls or glasses, cover with plastic wrap and refrigerate overnight.

Serve with a drizzle of cream, and fresh berries.

SERVES 4

spiced biscuits with iced tea

ICED TEA
2 teaspoons black tea leaves
1 tablespoon finely chopped lemongrass
90 g (3¼ oz/¼ cup) honey
fresh mint leaves

150 g (5½ oz) rice flour
50 g (1¾ oz) shallots
30 g (1 oz/⅓ cup) desiccated coconut
1 teaspoon sesame seeds
1 teaspoon nigella seeds
1 teaspoon poppy seeds
½ teaspoon fennel seeds
½ teaspoon ground cumin
1 egg white, whisked
250 ml (9 fl oz/1 cup) peanut oil

To make the iced tea, put the tea leaves and lemongrass into a large jug and add 1.5 litres (52 fl oz/6 cups) of boiling water. Allow to infuse for 5 minutes, then stir in the honey. Strain into another jug and chill until ready to use.

In a large frying pan, toast the rice flour over medium heat, stirring constantly. When it is golden brown remove from the heat and set aside.

Put the shallots and coconut into a blender with 125 ml (4 fl oz/½ cup) of water and process for a few minutes until smooth.

Put the toasted rice into a bowl and add the seeds, cumin, 1 teaspoon of sea salt, the coconut mixture and the egg white. Work the mixture into a dough, then with your hands roll it into small slightly flattened balls. Heat half the peanut oil in a deep frying pan or saucepan over medium heat and fry the biscuits a few at a time until golden brown. Add more oil as you need it. Drain the biscuits on paper towel and cool them on a wire rack. Store in an airtight container.

Pour the tea into glasses filled with ice and mint leaves, and serve with the biscuits.

BISCUIT RECIPE MAKES 20

extras

mix, match and complement

Everyone has their list of kitchen essentials and basics and, to be honest, mine varies a little with food trends and favourite ingredients. However, there are some store cupboard essentials you should always have, as well as a few surprise elements that will give a quick meal that desired extra pizzazz.

Always have fresh herbs and lemon to hand as they will lighten and refresh the flavours of any meal. To these fresh flavours add preserved lemon, salted capers, good quality olive oil, a few good stocks, mustard and some homestyle relishes and chilli jam. For substance, add tinned chickpeas and white beans, frozen berries and peas, potatoes, dried pasta, onions and garlic.

Chickpeas and white beans can bulk out a soup or salad, or can be heated and mashed for a quick side dish. Frozen peas are a perfect green fix when the crisper is bare, while frozen berries make a great standby dessert tossed into a crumble, scattered over puff pastry or simply spooned over ice cream.

With a few tricks like these up your culinary sleeve, you can make the most of seasonal produce and enjoy the moments you spend in the kitchen. The following pages also offer some basic recipes that can add substance and taste to many meals, as well as a glossary of common ingredients.

couscous

185 g (6½ oz/1 cup) instant couscous
20 g (¾ oz) butter
250 ml (9 fl oz/1 cup) boiling water

Put the couscous and butter in a large
bowl and pour the boiling water over the
top. Cover and allow to sit for 5 minutes,
then fluff up the grains with a fork. Cover
again and leave for a further 5 minutes.
Season with a little sea salt and freshly
ground black pepper, then rub the grains
with your fingertips to remove any lumps.
Serve warm or at room temperature.

SERVES 4 AS A SIDE DISH

ginger-spiced rice

2 tablespoons olive oil
4 shallots, finely chopped
½ teaspoon finely chopped fresh
    ginger
400 g (14 oz/2 cups) jasmine rice

Heat the olive oil in a saucepan and add
the chopped shallots. Sauté until soft, then
add the ginger, rice, 1 teaspoon of sea salt
and 1 litre (35 fl oz/4 cups) of water. Gently
bring to the boil, reduce the heat to low
and cover. Cook until all the liquid has
been absorbed.

SERVES 4–6

harissa

1 roasted red capsicum (pepper)
2 garlic cloves, roughly chopped
4 red chillies, seeded and roughly
    chopped
1 teaspoon ground coriander
1 teaspoon ground cumin
a handful of coriander (cilantro)
    leaves, roughly chopped
60 ml (2 fl oz/¼ cup) olive oil
1 tablespoon lemon juice

Remove any seeds, membrane and skin
from the roasted capsicum. Roughly chop
the flesh, put it in a food processor with the
remaining ingredients and process to
a thick sauce. Store in the refrigerator.

MAKES APPROXIMATELY ½ CUP

labne

200 g (7 oz/¾ cup) Greek-style
    yoghurt

Put the yoghurt into a muslin-lined strainer
over a bowl. Refrigerate overnight but do
not cover. Remove the thickened yoghurt in
heaped tablespoonfuls and roll into rough
balls. If not using straight away, marinate
the yoghurt balls in olive oil flavoured with
spices, garlic and lemon zest.

MAKES ABOUT 8 LABNE BALLS

mashed potato

1 kg (2 lb 4 oz) all-purpose potatoes
125 ml (4 fl oz/½ cup) milk
100 g (3½ oz) butter
pinch of ground white pepper

Peel the potatoes and cut them into
chunks. Put them in a large saucepan of
cold water, bring to the boil and cook for
30 minutes or until cooked through.
Meanwhile, put the milk and butter in a
small saucepan. Warm over low heat until
the butter has melted.

Drain the potato and return to the warm
pan. Mash the potato while it is still warm,
then whisk in the buttery milk until the
potato is soft and creamy. Season with sea
salt and white pepper.

SERVES 4–6 AS A SIDE DISH

mayonnaise

2 egg yolks
1 teaspoon Dijon mustard
1 tablespoon lemon juice
200 ml (7 fl oz) light olive oil

Whisk together the egg yolks, mustard and
lemon juice until light and creamy. Drizzle
in the olive oil, a little at a time, whisking
continuously until a thick mayonnaise
forms. Season to taste.

MAKES ABOUT 250 G (9 OZ/1 CUP)

polenta

1 teaspoon sea salt
250 g (9 oz/1⅔ cups) polenta
150 g (5½ oz/1½ cups) grated
    parmesan cheese
60 g (2¼ oz) butter

Bring 1.5 litres (52 fl oz/6 cups) of water to
the boil. Add the sea salt, then slowly pour
in the polenta while whisking. Reduce the
heat to low and cook for 40 minutes at a
gentle simmer, stirring from time to time.
Add the parmesan cheese and butter and
stir until incorporated.

SERVES 4–6 AS A SIDE DISH

roast potatoes

8 roasting potatoes (such as coliban
    or sebago)
olive oil, for drizzling

Preheat the oven to 200°C (400°F/Gas 6).
Peel the potatoes and cut them into
large chunks. Put the potato chunks in a
saucepan of cold salted water. Bring to the
boil and cook until the potatoes are almost
cooked through, but still firm on the outside.

Drain and put in a roasting tin, then run the
tines of a fork over the potatoes to give the
surface texture. Drizzle with olive oil, season
with sea salt and roast for 40 minutes or
until golden and crispy, turning the potatoes
at least once during cooking.

Or: Slice the washed new potatoes in half and toss with olive oil, sea salt and rosemary. Put the potatoes on a baking tray and roast for 30–40 minutes or until crisp, golden and cooked through.

SERVES 4 AS A SIDE DISH

roast tomatoes

roma (plum) tomatoes
caster (superfine) sugar, sea salt and
    freshly ground black pepper
    (as seasoning, to taste)
thyme sprigs (optional)
extra virgin olive oil and fresh basil
    leaves to serve

Preheat the oven to 150°C (300°F/Gas 2). Cut the required number of ripe roma tomatoes into halves or quarters. Put them on a baking tray, flesh side up and sprinkle lightly with caster (superfine) sugar, sea salt and freshly ground black pepper. You may like to add some thyme sprigs.

Bake for 1–2 hours or until the tomatoes are beginning to dry out and wrinkle up. Put the tomatoes in a serving dish and drizzle with extra virgin olive oil. Serve with a scatter of fresh basil leaves.

salsa verde

a handful of flat-leaf (Italian) parsley
10 mint leaves
1 garlic clove
3 anchovy fillets
35 g (1¼ oz/¼ cup) capers
1 teaspoon Dijon mustard
1 tablespoon lemon juice
80 ml (2½ fl oz/⅓ cup) extra virgin
    olive oil

Roughly chop the parsley with the mint, garlic, anchovy fillets and capers. Tip the chopped ingredients into a bowl and mix in the mustard, lemon juice and extra virgin olive oil. Store in the refrigerator.

MAKES APPROXIMATELY ½ CUP

shortcrust pastry

200 g (7 oz/1⅔ cups) plain
    (all-purpose) flour
100 g (3½ oz) chilled unsalted butter,
    cut into cubes
1 tablespoon caster (superfine) sugar
2 tablespoons chilled water

Put the flour, butter, sugar and a pinch of salt into a food processor and process for a minute. Add the chilled water and process until the mixture comes together. If necessary, add more water. Wrap the dough in plastic wrap and chill for 30 minutes.

Using a rolling pin, roll out the pastry working from the centre outwards, until it is approximately 3 mm (⅛ in) thick. The pastry can be rolled out on a floured surface, between two layers of plastic wrap or on baking paper. Use the pastry to line a 23 cm (9 in) flan (tart) tin. Chill for a further 30 minutes.

Preheat the oven to 180°C (350°F/Gas 4). Prick the base of the pastry case, line it with crumpled baking paper and fill with baking weights or uncooked rice. Bake the case for 10 minutes, or until the pastry looks cooked and dry. Remove from the oven, remove the baking paper and weights or rice, and return to the oven for a further couple of minutes or until the pastry is uniformly golden.

steamed white rice

200 g (7 oz/1 cup) white long-grain rice
435 ml (15¼ fl oz/1¾ cups) water

Rinse the rice under cold running water for a few minutes. Put the drained rice in a saucepan that has a tight-fitting lid. Cover the rice with the water and add a pinch of sea salt. Bring to the boil, then stir once to ensure the grains have not stuck to the base of the pan. Put the lid on the pan and turn the heat down to the lowest setting. Cook the rice for 15 minutes, then take the pan off the heat and allow the rice to sit, covered, for a further 10 minutes. Just before serving, fluff up the grains with a fork.

SERVES 2–4 AS A SIDE DISH

tahini dressing

135 g (4¾ oz/½ cup) tahini
1 tablespoon lemon juice
80 ml (2½ fl oz/⅓ cup) water
sea salt and ground white pepper

Put the tahini in a bowl and add the lemon juice. Stir several times, then add the water and continue to stir until smooth. Season to taste with sea salt and ground white pepper.

SERVES 4–6 AS A DIP

tapenade

80 g (2¾ oz) pitted kalamata olives
1 garlic clove, roughly chopped
a handful of flat-leaf (Italian) parsley, roughly chopped
10 basil leaves
2 anchovy fillets
1 teaspoon salted capers, rinsed
60 ml (2 fl oz/¼ cup) extra virgin olive oil

Put all the ingredients in a blender or food processor and blend to a rough paste. Season to taste with freshly ground black pepper. Store in the refrigerator.

MAKES APPROXIMATELY ½ CUP

glossary

arame

Arame is a Japanese seaweed which is commonly sold dried. When reconstituted it forms brown strands which have a mild, semi-sweet flavour and a firm texture.

balsamic vinegar

Balsamic vinegar is a dark, fragrant, sweetish aged vinegar made from grape juice. The production of authentic balsamic vinegar is carefully controlled. Bottles of the real thing are labelled Aceto Balsamico Tradizionale de Modena, while commercial varieties simply have Aceto Balsamico de Modena. Caramelised balsamic vinegar, available from most speciality food stores, is a sweetened reduction that is thicker, sweeter and less acidic than regular balsamic vinegar.

bocconcini

These are small balls of fresh mozzarella cheese, often sold sitting in their own whey. When fresh they are soft and springy to the touch and have a milky taste. They are available from most delicatessens and supermarkets.

buffalo mozzarella

A soft creamy white mozzarella cheese traditionally made in southern Italy. It is considered to be the best quality mozzarella due to its texture and flavour.

caperberries

Caperberries are the fruits of the caper plant and are normally found pickled in jars with their stems attached. They have a slightly milder flavour to the caper. They can be found in most supermarkets and delicatessens.

chocolate

Couverture is the best quality chocolate. This bittersweet chocolate contains the highest percentage of cocoa butter and is sold in good delicatessens and food stores. If you are unable to obtain chocolate of this standard, then it is preferable to use a good quality eating chocolate rather than a cheap cooking chocolate. Cooking chocolates, on the whole, do not have a good flavour and tend to result in an oily rather than a buttery texture.

daikon

Daikon, also known as mooli, is a large white radish. Its flavour varies from mild to surprisingly spicy depending on the season and variety. It can be freshly grated in salads or slow-cooked in broths, and is available from most large supermarkets or Asian grocery stores. Select firm vegetables with unscarred skins.

dried Asian fried shallots

Crisp-fried shallots or onions are available from most Asian grocery stores and are normally packaged in plastic tubs or bags.

They are used as a flavour enhancer, scattered over rice and savoury dishes.

enoki mushrooms

These pale delicate mushrooms have a long thin stalk and tiny caps. They are very fragile and need only a minimal cooking time. They are bland in flavour but have an interesting texture and appearance, so are ideal for blending with other mushrooms or for using in stir-fries to add an interesting texture.

fish sauce

This pungent, salty liquid made from fermented fish is widely used in South-East Asian cooking to add a salty, savoury flavour. Buy a small bottle and store it in the refrigerator.

fresh horseradish

Horseradish is a large white root of the mustard family. It is very pungent and has a spicy, hot flavour. It is usually freshly grated as a condiment for roast beef and smoked fish. When commercially produced, horseradish is often blended with cream to give it a smoother texture.

gelatine

Gelatine is a setting agent used for making jellies, desserts and for glazing. It is available in a powdered form or in leaves, which are soaked in cold water before use. The leaves are easier to use but the powdered form is commonly found in supermarkets. Always follow the manufacturer's instructions, which follow a simple ratio of liquid to setting agent.

goat's curd

This is a soft, fresh cheese made from goat's milk. It has a slightly acidic but mild and creamy flavour.

harissa

A spicy red paste flavoured with chillies and spices. It is traditionally used as a condiment in North African cuisine. It can be made fresh (see page 241) or can be bought in most delicatessens or large supermarkets.

kecap manis

Kecap manis is an Indonesian soy sauce which is darker, thicker and sweeter than normal soy sauce. It can be found in the Asian section of large supermarkets or specialty Asian stores.

labne / labna

Labne is a simple cream cheese made from salted yoghurt (see recipe page 241). It is traditionally served at breakfast with bread.

miso paste

An important ingredient in Japanese cooking, miso paste is made of fermented soya beans and other ingredients including wheat, rice and barley. It is used as a flavouring in soups and stews, or as a condiment.

orange flower water

This perfumed distillation of bitter-orange blossoms is mostly used as a flavouring in desserts and drinks. It is available from large supermarkets and delicatessens.

passata

A rich, thick tomato purée made from sieved tomatoes. It can be used as a base in sauces and soups.

preserved lemon

These are whole lemons preserved in salt or brine, which turns their rind soft and pliable. Only the rind is used in cooking—the pulp should be scraped out and discarded. Available from delicatessens and large supermarkets.

ras al hanout

A classic spice blend used in Moroccan cooking. The name means 'top of the shop' or the very best spice blend that a spice merchant has to offer. It contains a varied selection of spices, including paprika, cumin, ginger, coriander seed, allspice, cardamom and nutmeg. Available from the spice section of most large supermarkets.

rosewater

A natural flavouring made from the essence of rose petals, it is commonly used to flavour Middle Eastern and Indian desserts, drinks and confectionery. It can be found in most supermarkets or specialty food stores.

saffron threads

The orange-red stigmas from one species of crocus plant, saffron threads are the most expensive spice in the world. Each flower consists of three stigmas, which are hand-picked, then dried—a labour-intensive process. Saffron should be bought in small quantities and used sparingly as it has a very strong flavour.

salsa verde

Salsa verde or green sauce is a type of dressing made from finely chopped parsley, garlic, lemon juice and olive oil (see page 243). Commonly flavoured with capers, anchovies or mint, it is used as a dressing for seafood and cooked vegetables. You can make your own or buy it from supermarkets.

salted capers

These are the green buds from a Mediterranean shrub, preserved in brine or salt. Salted capers have a firmer texture and are often smaller than those preserved in brine. Rinse away the salt or brine before using them. Salted capers are available from good delicatessens.

shiitake mushrooms

These Asian mushrooms have white gills and a brown cap. Meaty in texture, they keep their shape when cooked. Dried shiitake are often sold as dried Chinese mushrooms.

soba noodles

These thin buckwheat noodles make an ideal base for Asian-style noodle salads or soups. They are usually sold dried and are sometimes flavoured with green tea.

sour cherries

Sour or morello cherries are most commonly sold bottled in sweet juice and are available from most supermarkets. They have a slightly tart flavour, making them ideal for baking.

star anise

This is a pretty, star-shaped dried fruit containing small, oval, brown seeds. Star anise has a flavour similar to anise, but is more liquorice-like. It is commonly used whole because of its decorative shape.

sumac

Sumac is a peppery, sour spice made from dried and ground sumac berries. The fruit of a northern hemisphere shrub, sumac is widely used in Middle Eastern cookery. It is available from most large supermarkets and Middle Eastern speciality stores.

tahini

This is a thick, creamy paste made from husked and ground white sesame seeds. It is used to give a strong nutty flavour to Middle Eastern salads, sauces and dips. Tahini is available in jars from health food stores and most supermarkets.

tamarind

Tamarind is the sour pulp of an Asian fruit. It is most commonly available compressed into cakes or refined as tamarind concentrate in jars. Tamarind concentrate is widely available; the pulp can be found in Asian food shops.

tofu

This white curd is made from soya beans and is a great source of protein. Tofu is usually sold in blocks and comes in several different grades—soft (silken), firm, sheets and deep-fried. Refrigerate fresh tofu covered in water for up to five days, changing the water daily.

vanilla bean

The long, slim black vanilla bean has a wonderful caramel aroma which synthetic vanillas can never capture. Good quality beans are soft and not too dry. Store unused vanilla beans in a full jar of caster (superfine) sugar—this will help keep the vanilla fresh, and the aroma of the bean will also quickly infuse the sugar, making it a wonderful addition to desserts and baking.

vanilla extract

When using vanilla extract, always ensure it is made from real vanilla and is not labelled 'imitation' vanilla extract or essence. The flavours are quite different, with the imitation being almost acrid in its aftertaste. See also vanilla bean.

index

Acknowledgments

This may be a book about fresh and easy food, but I do still have many people to thank for bringing such a beautiful book to completion.

I'd like to start with Murdoch Books, and in particular Kay Scarlett and Juliet Rogers, for allowing me to work on the marie claire series. Thank you once again. A big thank you to Desney King and Daniela Bertollo for their editorial eye and for cracking the whip when necessary. Thanks also to Holly Henderson and Erika Cvejik for all their assistance. A huge thank you to Vivien Valk for finding 'the garden', sharing the fun and turning it all into a gorgeous book.

The girls and boys in the test kitchen did a fantastic job of testing the recipes and making queries whenever it was necessary. Thanks to all, for your honesty and assistance.

Cathy Armstrong came to my rescue and helped in the long process of writing and testing recipes. Thank you for your generosity with concepts and ideas and for being such an inspiring friend. Heidi Flett was once more the angel in the kitchen. Thank you so much for all the beautiful food, yummy lunches and fun times in the studio.

Margot Braddon has again brought her fabulous and quirky style to this book. She has re-created the garden with flowers and embroidery, craft and colour. Thank you so much for a month of creative fun and a book of beautiful images. Thanks also to Yuji, Hanako and Bridget for their help in the studio and a big thanks to Gerrie for the constant flow of caffeine.

This is a book of food and flowers, smiles and sunshine and for that I have to thank our two wonderful photographers. Gorta Yuuki brought his quiet humour and considered eye to the studio. Thank you so much for the beautiful light and sparkling food. In the garden, Anthony Ong has once again cast a spell over all of us. His beautiful shots of Stephanie, Mariana and Letisha have given the book its sunny life. A very big thank you must also go to Jan and Peter for lending us their exquisite garden and giving this book such a beautiful backdrop. My thanks also to Katrina Raftery for sprinkling the girls with a little fairy dust. And a huge thank you to Kim Payne for the gorgeous wardrobe and lifestyle styling.

Lastly, I'd like to thank my family of boys who every day provide me with equal parts sunshine and joy, despite the fact that they often have to share the house with me and 'the book'.

Thank you all, for everything.

Published in 2011 by Murdoch Books Pty Limited

Murdoch Books Australia
Pier 8/9
23 Hickson Road
Millers Point NSW 2000
Phone: +61 (0) 2 8220 2000
Fax: +61 (0) 2 8220 2558
www.murdochbooks.com.au

Murdoch Books UK Limited
Erico House, 6th Floor
93–99 Upper Richmond Road
Putney, London SW15 2TG
Phone: +44 (0) 20 8785 5995
Fax: +44 (0) 20 8785 5985
www.murdochbooks.co.uk

Publisher: Kylie Walker
Photographers: Anthony Ong (lifestyle) and Gorta Yuuki (food)
Stylists: Kim Payne (lifestyle) and Margot Braddon (food)
Models: Stephanie Eales, Letisha Gibara, Mariana, from Chic Management
Editor: Desney King
Design and art direction: Vivien Valk
Food preparation: Heidi Flett
Production: Joan Beal

National Library of Australia Cataloguing-in-Publication Data

Author: Cranston, Michele.
Title: Marie Claire fresh + easy / Michele Cranston.
ISBN: 978-1-74196-549-0 (pbk.)
Notes: Includes index.
Subject: Cookery.
Dewey Number: 641.6383

A catalogue record for this book is available from the British Library.

Printed by 1010 Printing International Limited in 2011. PRINTED IN CHINA.

The publisher and stylists would like to thank Collector Store, Newspaper Taxi, Koskela Design, The Society Inc, Bough of
Bondi Markets and The Bronte Tram for their generous loans of props. Thanks also to Bradley Perkins from Company 1 for
his generous assistance and cooperation.

IMPORTANT: Those who might be at risk from the effects of salmonella poisoning (the elderly, pregnant women, young
children and those suffering from immune deficiency diseases) should consult their doctor with any concerns about
eating raw eggs.

CONVERSION GUIDE: You may find cooking times vary depending on the oven you are using. For fan-forced ovens, as a
general rule, set the oven temperature to 20°C (35°F) lower than indicated in the recipe. We have used 20 ml (4 teaspoon)
tablespoon measures. If you are using a 15 ml (3 teaspoon) tablespoon, for most recipes the difference will not be
noticeable. However, for recipes using baking powder, gelatine, bicarbonate of soda (baking soda), small amounts of flour
and cornflour (cornstarch), add an extra teaspoon for each tablespoon specified.